SELL YOUR START-UP

THE FOUNDER'S GUIDE TO NAVIGATE AND WIN AT M&A

SYEDA NAZIFA NAWROJ, ESQ.

Difference Press

Washington DC, USA

Copyright © Syeda Nazifa Nawroj, 2024

Published 2024

DISCLAIMER

accuracy, or effectiveness of the information provided herein. The legal and economic landscapes are constantly evolving, both within the Unites States and internationally, and laws and regulations may also evolve and change after the publication of this book. The author expressly disclaims any and all responsibility for any errors or omissions herein or for any outcomes related to or in connection with the use of the information herein.

This book is not intended to replace the advice of a legal or any other professional, regardless of whether they are certified or licensed. The author unequivocally recommends that you consult with a lawyer, or other applicable professional advisor, before making any decisions based on any content in this book.

Cover design: Jennifer Stimson

Editing: Madeline Kosten

Author photo courtesy of: Chitoh Yung

PRAISE FOR
SYEDA NAZIFA NAWROJ, ESQ.

"*Sell Your Start-Up* by Syeda Nazifa Nawroj, Esq. is an insightful and accessible guide for start-up founders navigating the complexities of mergers and acquisitions. With a unique focus on underserved entrepreneurs, Nawroj expertly blends legal expertise with practical advice, making this a must-read for those looking to successfully sell their business while safeguarding their vision and legacy. A valuable resource for any founder preparing for their first M&A experience."

— KASHIF ZUBAIR, CEO, AMCOB –
ALLIED MUSLIM CHAMBER OF
BUSINESS

"This book covers every step of the selling process, from finding the right buyer to closing the deal. Nawroj provides a comprehensive guide for any founder looking to maximize their exit. Highly recommend it."

— NIRVIKAR JAIN, MANAGING
DIRECTOR & FINTECH LEAD,
WOODSIDE CAPITAL PARTNERS

"Nawroj lays down a roadmap and then systematically walks you through the lifecycle of an M&A transaction from beginning to end. The magic of this book is how easy it is to read and how simple she makes this complex topic feel. Excited to read it again one day when I'm selling my company."

— BRIAN SCHERER ESQ, CEO,
HEYCOUNSEL

To my husband, Ahsan, who negotiated expertly to win this dedication;
To my child, Zikr, who did nothing for it but still also won this dedication; and
To my father, Inamul, and my mother, Raihana, who taught me that it's not about winning
but about service to our fellow human beings.
Each of you make me a better negotiator and an even better human. Thank you.

CONTENTS

FOREWORD

When I first entered the world of start-ups, I quickly learned that while building a business from the ground up is exhilarating, navigating the complexities of scaling, fundraising, and ultimately, mergers and acquisitions (M&A) can be daunting. As a two-time Y Combinator-backed founder, having experience with venture fundraising for my start-ups, setting up the process for an exit to my first start-up, and advising start-ups on M&A deals, I've seen firsthand how crucial it is to have a deep understanding...

The truth is, many entrepreneurs don't think about M&A until they're already in the middle of it – or worse, scrambling at the last minute. This is where *Sell Your Start-Up* comes in. It serves as a glossary of essential terms and concepts that every founder should have a grasp of long before they step into negotiations. Whether you're looking at M&A as an exit strategy or a growth mechanism, having this foundational knowledge is a game-changer.

In my experience advising start-ups, particularly in helping them through M&A processes, I've seen how much difference preparedness can make. Being able to demystify M&A jargon and anticipate the next steps not only makes the process smoother but also allows founders to stay in control, ensuring they don't leave value on the table.

What I appreciate most about *Sell Your Start-Up* is its accessibility. It doesn't bog you down with dense technical jargon but provides a comprehensive guide to understanding M&A in a way that is both insightful and actionable. It's the perfect starting point for anyone looking to educate themselves before embarking on an acquisition journey, whether you're a first-time founder or a seasoned entrepreneur.

From understanding purchase prices and risk allocation to preparing your company for sale and negotiating a letter of intent, this guide covers every critical aspect of the M&A process. It provides you with the insights you need to make informed decisions and avoid common pitfalls. If I had access to a book like this when I was first navigating M&A, it would have saved me many sleepless nights and countless hours of research.

For any founder considering M&A, this book is an indispensable tool. It allows you to approach your business sale with confidence, ensuring that you not only survive the process but thrive in it. I highly recommend reading *Sell Your Start-Up* cover to cover and keeping it close throughout your M&A journey.

— ANISA MIRZA, 2X Y COMBINATOR-
BACKED FOUNDER | START-UP
ADVISOR

WELCOME TO M&A

RECENT M&A ACTIVITY

I t is my great pleasure to welcome you to the world of mergers and acquisitions (M&A), a realm where businesses are bought and sold, creating opportunities for growth, transformation, and generational wealth. This chapter provides you with a bird's-eye view of this realm of M&A, with a focus on selling the control of private companies in the technology (and other loosely related) industries. This book is especially helpful for founders who are about to navigate their first company sale and anyone with curiosity about this highly impactful corporate industry.

Many businesspeople do not realize how big the M&A market is – which is measured in total transaction value. I am practicing M&A and writing this book during an unprecedented and tumultuous time in the history of M&A activity.

At the start of the pandemic in 2020, the economic uncertainty caused global M&A activity to slump to $3.1 trillion (yes, "trillion" with a t!) in total transaction value from $3.7 trillion in 2019. The United States is the largest market where M&A activity occurs, with more than half of all M&A deals in the world – both domestic and international – occurring here. The US M&A activity tracked a similar slump with global M&A activity in 2020, falling to $1.8 trillion from nearly $2 trillion in 2019. However, as the pandemic wore on, storefront businesses shuttered while online businesses flourished. The sale of both distressed and successful companies fuelled a record-breaking M&A activity recovery in 2021. Global M&A activity rose to a whopping all-time high of $5.9 trillion in total transaction value while US M&A activity soared to $2.6 trillion.

I had the great privilege of being at the forefront of this M&A activity boom – fueled by technology companies – as an associate at the premier Silicon Valley law firm Fenwick & West LLP. At Fenwick, I worked on industry-leading transactions, such as the sale of ThousandEyes to Cisco for approximately $900 million and the sale of Streamlit to Snowflake for $800 million. It was a thrilling time to be in sell-side technology M&A.

In 2022, the global M&A market took a precipitous plunge of 52 percent from $5.9 trillion in 2021 to $2.8 trillion in 2022 and kept falling – though less steeply – at 16 percent to $2.5 trillion in 2023. In the United States, M&A activity dropped to its lowest proportion of the S&P 500 market value in twenty years in 2023. As the post-pandemic disruption began to soften, dampening economic factors slowly piled up, causing M&A activity to decline. In the United States, interest rates crept up, raising the costs of financing an acquisition. Both the European Union and the Biden-Harris administration in the United States began to crack down on very large M&A deals by finding potential antitrust violations after decades of lenient administrative oversight. Political unrest began to spread across the globe. I continued doing

M&A work throughout this downturn, but the landscape had changed. Private company valuations were lower, with potential acquirers renegotiating the letter of intent (or LOI) over and over, looking to pay less each time. More of the M&A activity entailed sales of distressed companies or at lower-than-expected valuations. More deals were structured as asset sales instead of mergers where companies sought to divest of cost-centers or sell off business assets or divisions to raise capital. The deals got smaller and harder to close.

In 2024, M&A activity has started picking up slowly, but steadily, and I expect M&A activity to continue to grow. M&A is perceived to be one of the most vital strategic levers for inorganic business growth by business leaders, so savvy founders are planning to use this as a business tool among many others. Additionally, there is a lot of dry powder in private coffers waiting to be invested – private fund administrators are just being more cautious, and more discerning given the state of the US and global economy, which increases the likelihood of start-ups failing. Founders and their businesses need to know how to posture their companies ideally in order to tap into this ever-increasing pool of private capital.

SMALL TO MIDSIZE M&A

I operate in the small to midsize M&A deal space, largely involving the sale of private companies in the United States (to other private companies or to public companies). There are a great many transactions of various types that take place in this slice of the economy, both globally and here at home. However, much of it doesn't get reported, and therefore, they don't get included in the M&A activity that is thereafter shared with us. Most of the data we have on M&A relates to public companies, because such companies have certain obligations to disclose material transactions to stockholders in the public stock exchange markets. However, private companies don't have such disclosure obligations and often don't report deals voluntarily, choosing to keep their M&A activity confidential since it could tip the hand on their competitive business strategies. As a result, most available statistics on M&A are for deals over the value of $25 million and where public companies were involved. Many smaller M&A deals, and large deals between private companies, take place all the time without being reported or shared. As a result, there is a dearth of reliable information on private company M&A activity and on what's "market" in this slice of our economy.

Of the little information available on private company M&A, much comes from lawyers, like myself, and other M&A practitioners who choose to share their knowledge and experiences.

One informative study on private target M&A is done by the M&A Sub-Committee of the American Bar Association (ABA). The latest Private Target M&A Deal Points Study by the ABA, just published in September 2024, analyzes publicly available acquisition agreements for transactions for which definitive agreements were executed or completed in 2022 and the first quarter of 2023 that involved private targets being acquired by public companies. The study presents data on 108 such deals ranging in value from $30 million to $750 million and identifies the top three industries in this market: technology, healthcare, and financial services. I refer to this study throughout the book as the 2023 ABA M&A Deal Points Study.

Even among M&A practitioners, especially in the private

company M&A space, much of the research and literature, in addition to being dense, is written from a neutral perspective or with a view toward advising buyers in an M&A. Such writers believe it's a good idea to focus their advice on, or at least make it useful for, the party in the transaction holding the purse strings. That is understandable but not my goal here.

While buyers might hold the purse-strings, it is the sellers, and the constituent, or target companies, that bring the multiples of value that all parties seek in an M&A.

As an advocate for start-up founders in general, I have a particular fondness for advising founders to realize the most value for their businesses. I love to fight and win at M&A on the sell side for the start-up founder, and this book is an indulgence in my fancy. Unlike most M&A books, this book is written with the start-up founder in mind and biased toward guiding sellers, and the constituent or the target companies, in an M&A transaction.

IDENTIFYING MY IDEAL READER

You might be plagued with indecision about whether, when, or how to sell your company. In my experience practicing M&A in Silicon Valley, a lot of start-up founders selling a company for the first time are woefully unprepared to take advantage of this once-in-a-lifetime opportunity to win big. This occurs despite the free market's best efforts. When the start-up is at its nascent stages, founders have to fight tooth and nail just to survive: 10 percent of all start-ups fail within their first year of formation, and thereafter, 90 percent of all

start-ups are defunct within the first five years of their formation. Just surviving is a mean feat. On top of this, the start-up
failure rates are highest among first-time founders. With such
a steep climb, most founders are advised to focus on reaching
the peak value for their business instead of getting distracted
with potential exit plans.

**This means that successful start-up founders
happen to walk into, or get pushed into, M&A
deals instead of intentionally entering into
them with purpose.**

This also means that founders of start-ups that are not
doing so hot struggle to grow until vultures swoop in to pick
apart the start-up for parts. None of these outcomes have to be
your destiny. For you, M&A can be a powerful tool in your
business toolkit that you wield with purpose to further your
business objectives.

I have represented many founders across various different
types of M&A deals over the years and want to introduce you
to a typical start-up founder, Sarah. Sarah is an amalgamation
of many different clients I have represented over the years and
is imaginary. I will use her journey to illustrate how the lack
of information on private company M&A could affect a start-
up founder's experience with engaging in an M&A in real
life.

MEET SARAH: AN IMAGINARY YET TYPICAL CLIENT

Sarah is a thirty-eight-year-old start-up founder living in
Oakland, California, with her partner. She holds a BS in elec-
trical engineering from Stanford University and a PhD in
robotics from UC Berkeley. She came to the United States

with a full scholarship from China that she worked all her young teenage life to earn. Sarah wanted to come to the United States for the incredible innovation opportunities here.

During her PhD program, Sarah thought of an idea to make prosthetics more suitable for children. As part of her PhD thesis, she proposed a method to print prosthetic parts cheaply using a 3D printer so they are adaptable and can grow as the child grows. UC Berkeley helped get Sarah a joint patent with the university for her unique method of 3D printing prosthetic parts. After her PhD, Sarah wanted to start her own company using her patented method to bring flexible and affordable prosthetics to handicapped children. Her parents were opposed; they wanted Sarah to get a stable job at Apple or Google. However, Sarah's vision and purpose were stronger. She overcame her cultural anxiety because her mission to help these children trumped her discomfort.

Over the next couple of years, Sarah struggled greatly to get venture financing in Silicon Valley. She needed funding to negotiate a license with the university to use the existing patent and to also work on new technology to grow her patent portfolio. Sarah didn't have much money herself and didn't come from wealth, so she didn't know wealthy friends or family who could act as angel investors. As an immigrant, she was also under the constant threat of losing her immigration status. Her schools, though, were amazing networks of peers and experts who could help advise and guide her.

She begged and pleaded to investor after investor and had many doors shut in her face. Less than 2 percent of venture financing goes to women founders and possibly even less to immigrants and persons of color (no reported numbers on this). Sarah was told she was too young, too inexperienced in business, or too *insert your reason of choice*. She relied on the kindness and generosity of her friends and colleagues who let her crash on their couches and introduced her to helpful contacts. Sarah held a few jobs here and there to live but never gave up on her dream because her mission was bigger than her needs.

Finally, Sarah caught a break when she was pitching her business idea for the hundredth time at a college shark tank. She got enough funding from an angel investor to get a license from the university, hire a team, and start manufacturing prosthetics in China. A company was born. Her team continued to innovate and filed for more patents over time. After a few years of grinding away, Sarah's vision seemed to catch on overnight. Her products started selling like hotcakes and she began profitably licensing her prosthetics designs. Suddenly, there was no shortage of investors who believed in her – now that the worst of it was over. She was able to raise a substantial Series A financing round. Organizations began to invite her to speak at events, and she was recognized as a 40-under-40 innovator in her industry. Sarah's business was finally taking off, and even her parents were coming around!

One day, out of the blue, one of Sarah's venture investors called her and said he knew someone who was interested in buying her company. The price could be in the millions! However, the highly motivated buyer wants to sign and close a deal fast due to their internal financial targets. Could Sarah give him a response within twenty-four hours on whether she was willing to entertain the offer? Could Sarah also call a special meeting of the board of directors immediately so that he could share this offer with the board for their consideration? Otherwise, the buyer might move on to one of her competitors. What?!?

Sarah told her investor she would get back to him ASAP and hung up. She didn't know what to do. Sarah had dreamed at times about what she could do if she had money. Buy a house in a good school district in the Bay Area. Start a family. Multiply the good she has to offer to the world. This sale could be so great! However, Sarah was unsure if she was ready to part with her business yet. She had great plans for the next three, five, ten years to transform the lives of millions of children around the world by bringing them affordable prosthetics that grows with them. It's been her dream for too long, built in reality with blood, sweat, and tears. She didn't want to abandon it. Sarah had so many questions about this potential M&A offer.

Unlike starting the business, for which she already had a problem she was motivated to solve and had some idea of how to prepare solutions, she didn't know the first thing about selling her business. Also, this is so much more than a business to Sarah. This is a consequential and pivotal decision in her career and her life, and she has so little time to act on it. What should she do?

COMMON CONCERNS FOR FOUNDERS

If you are a start-up founder like Sarah, you may now be considering your options.

First, you may leverage your professional network and call on business contacts. However, it's unlikely their M&A experience would be a comprehensive guide to navigate yours because each M&A transaction is unique. Each party in the transaction has one or more of their own objectives that they are aiming to achieve through the M&A. You, like Sarah, could be aiming for a payday for your hard work in the past and the continued opportunity to grow the business according to your vision. In the M&A deal that is struck, both yours and the buyer's incentives have to align. Also, each party brings their own particular characteristics to the M&A that shape the deal. If Sarah's company is a Delaware C corporation head-quartered in California, then different rules would apply to it than if Sarah's company were the result of a joint venture between a California corporation owning the intellectual property and a company in China owning the manufacturing arm of the business. You may know a friend who has sold their company to a private equity fund and walked away with a hefty parachute payment, now living most of their time on an estate in Hawaii. However, that friend's M&A experience may not be a reliable guide because of the uniqueness of their M&A.

Second, you need to treat M&A as sensitive business. You may be barred under law and contract from discussing any potential offers on the table to acquire your start-up with anyone other than an insider or confidential advisor to your business. If your buyer is a public company, then you need to follow securities laws and ensure there are no leaks that could affect the stock market for the buyer. Many M&As never closed due to market leaks that affected public company stock prices. Also, if word gets around that you are considering an M&A, more buyers might come out of the woodwork. Alter-natively, no other buyers might come forth and the potential deal on the table may not close – this could harm your good-will in the market and your start-up could end up being valued for less in the future. You, and Sarah, are constrained by these obligations incentivizing you to share potential M&A news of your start-up only on a need-to-know-basis. Whoever you speak to about a potential M&A offer should be savvy about the rules and market norms governing M&A to mini-mize any potential harm to you and your start-up.

Third, you may contact an M&A lawyer. You can call the corporate lawyers you hired in the past to raise venture funding to advise you or refer you to M&A lawyers they know. This seems like a great idea. However, let's be honest. Do you really like your corporate lawyer? Many underserved founders – women, immigrants, black people, indigenous people, people of color, LGBTQ+ and any other traditionally marginalized peoples in corporate America – often feel taken advantage of by their big firm lawyers. I had a client once tell me they were ghosted by the big law partner after he signed them on: he passed them on to his associates and later sent an inexplicably large bill that included costs for training said associates. I had another client tell me that their big firm partner had opted to address the more senior, white man who was chairman of the board of directors of her start-up instead of engaging with her – a young woman of color – as the chief executive officer (CEO). She felt that the partner thought her too young and didn't think it worth his while to bring her up to speed on the legal concept under negotiation. Even after paying the high fees these law firms charge, many diverse founders feel that their corporate lawyer does not believe in their potential or root for them as a dedicated business advisor should. Overall, it's possible that you, like Sarah, may not want to entrust the corporate lawyers you know with the sensitive business of your M&A.

But let's say that you did love your start-up lawyer. Yay! So, you decide to call her for advice and she connects you with an M&A lawyer. You know that M&A lawyers are famously expensive. They will likely charge you hundreds of dollars for a short consultation. You will feel hesitant about asking them to explain in detail or be subject to Q&A about the new and complicated concepts you are encountering in the M&A. You are billed by the hour for any time the lawyer spends on your matter so you are disincentivized from utilizing your lawyer's expertise and learning from them.

Even if you receive one or more free consultations and you are satisfied, you may wonder if your M&A lawyer can really understand your unique situation in time to give you useful feedback. Most importantly, selling your company is such a big decision for you. A large part of it is not even about the money. Will a corporate lawyer who does not know you or relate with you take the time or make the effort to coach you through the experience?

The reason why I refer to traditionally marginalized peoples in corporate America as underserved is because their unique needs are not typically catered to by big law firms. As an example, most big law firms with M&A shops have a tax lawyer specializing in executive compensation who can advise US persons on the tax consequences that a particular transaction type could have on them. However, most such firms do not have an immigration lawyer to advise a non-US founder or an immigrant to the United States about the effects of a transaction type on their immigration status and will expect the non-US founder to problem-solve on their own. Despite knowing (at least anecdotally), immigrants have proven to be extremely resilient, and therefore ultimately successful, founders in the United States, big law firms willing to take their money aren't as inclined to cater to their needs. I can think of many such traditionally underserved demographics.

Regardless of your unique circumstances, immigration or otherwise, there are surely some characteristics that you share with all start-up founders facing an M&A.

MY IDEAL READER

As a start-up founder, you most likely have significant ownership in a private company (whose shares or ownership are not listed or traded in a public stock exchange) in the small to midsize market space. As a start-up founder, you are also likely a director serving on the board of directors of your private company and you have fiduciary duties toward your stockholders. As a start-up founder, if you are still involved with the day-to-day operations of the company, you are also likely a chief executive officer (CEO), chief technology officer (CTO), or other key officer managing a critical business function who holds that office while being a full-time employee of the company. In an M&A, all of these roles that you play in the success of your company are called on, and each role is subject to diligence, negotiation, and "deal-making." This means you are intricately involved in an M&A as a founding stockholder, a director, an officer, and an employee. This book is written for you.

WELCOMING THE IDEAL READER

Since my very first deal and throughout the many M&A deals that followed, I became better and better at M&A as each unique transaction brought experience and insights. I began to discover that my wish for start-up founders is that they would know more about M&A generally before embarking on one. With some more insight into the M&A process, start-up founders could better navigate and win at M&A.

M&A is a realm of its own that pulls the many and varied threads across an entire business into a single transaction that fundamentally alters the business by changing its owners.

Many of my sell-side clients, especially those selling their company for the first time, had numerous questions about basic concepts and processes in M&A. However, by the time

they engaged an M&A lawyer at firms like DLA Piper or
Fenwick & West, the hourly billable rates were astronomical.
As a mid-level corporate M&A associate at Fenwick & West
in California, my time was billed to clients at around $850
per hour, while partners generally charged $1,200 or more
per hour. At smaller start-up law firms like Legal Scale LLP in
New York, my time was billed at about $650 per hour. Essen-
tially, M&A lawyers can be quite expensive. At these rates,
clients were often terrified to ask questions, constantly
watching the clock, fearing that their questions would simply
lead to more expensive bills.

This fear, coupled with the immense pressure of an M&A
deal, added to their stress. The M&A process itself can be
intensely stressful – your business is under extreme scrutiny,
all of your life's work is assessed, poked, and prodded, and you
are expected to negotiate the sale of your company in addition
to continuing to run your business (up until the sale or even
after closing, if the founder stays on as part of the deal). It's a
lot to ask of a person. Clients who were not fully aware of the
overall process and did not feel free to ask questions were
under even more stress. As I represented such clients in deal
after deal, the idea to write a book slowly began to form.

I wanted to write this book as a guide for anyone in the
shoes of a start-up founder looking to sell their company. I
want you to understand – at a very high level – how an M&A
works. What the basic stages of an M&A are and why they are
significant. What are the big issues that will affect value and
risk, and that you will need to address when negotiating such
a deal? Who are the vendors and players in this M&A industry, and how do you decide whether to engage their services?
These are all questions I have seen my clients ask in various
shapes and forms over the years. I wanted this book to be a
reliable, accessible answer to some of their core questions

from a former big firm M&A lawyer without the price tag of one.

I hope that after reading this book, you will no longer think of the process as a big, black box. My hope is that you will begin to understand some of the key concepts, processes, dynamics, and incentives at play in an M&A deal so that you do not feel completely lost and alone as you embark on the exciting and rewarding journey of selling your company. You may even be inspired to actively use M&A as a part of your business strategy.

Finally, I wrote this book to present an alternative idea of an M&A lawyer. It's hard to imagine a brown, female, immigrant mother as an M&A lawyer in the corporate world. Studies indicate that M&A law (along with maritime shipping law) has one of the lowest numbers of women and people of color as legal practitioners. This book is an attempt to prove to myself and to you that your M&A lawyer can be a regular someone you pass by at Target.

The next chapter provides details on my professional journey and background. This book is as much a campaign for diversity as it is an accessible educational endeavor. I hope my background inspires readers to engage more with M&A – an excellent source of building generational wealth – and to realize that people like me are here to help them in this space.

The approach and insights I include in this book are unique to me. You will surely find many fine practitioners in M&A who may disagree with some or many aspects of what I write. That is intentional. I am not writing this book to blend in with the existing M&A world but to stand out. This book is also not a comprehensive survey of basic concepts. Practically speaking, it's not possible to write a readable M&A book that includes all the concepts you would need to know. My intention is to make M&A more accessible to founders and businesses – not to be the luxury good that many in big law firms claim it to be. Reaping the rewards of building a successful business should not be a luxury – it should be commonplace.

I want your start-up to survive and be wildly successful. Once you are past the bare survival mode, think of M&A to grow your business. Even if you are struggling to survive, think of M&A as a tool you can use to partner up and save, get much-needed capital, or diversify into more resilient markets. This book is for you if you don't know much about M&A but want to begin using it as a tool in your business decision-making. Like many start-up founders, you may not have the time to get an MBA or a law degree, or the money to hire these graduates with high billable rates, to imbue you with the needed knowledge and expertise. You want a straightforward, easy-to-digest, and easy-to-implement guidebook to selling your company. This is that book.

2

KNOW YOUR AUTHOR, AN M&A LAWYER

MY WELCOME TO M&A

I still vividly remember the very first M&A deal that I ever managed (not just worked on but orchestrated). As a second-year associate, I was thrown into the deep end to negotiate and close the sale of a California private company for approximately $35 million based on a rudimentary letter of intent (LOI). It was a life sciences product design and manufacturing company headquartered in Santa Clara, California, that was largely owned by a husband-and-wife dynamic duo. The goal for the owners was to sell their company to a private equity fund and finally retire in comfort.

The owners were in their sixties and had been running the company for the greater part of three decades. They had built a small but loyal team of employees who had chosen to stay with the company for a long time, a decade or more for some of them. It was clear that this company was the owners' life's work, nurtured and grown with as much care as one might raise their own children. I took this responsibility very seriously and worked hard to make a deal that the owners could be proud of and one that would be a fitting end to their legacy.

A week before we were scheduled to close the deal, I got rear-ended by a speeding driver on a California highway on my home from work and got a concussion. I called my clients that evening and walked them through each and every detail to ensure that they felt comfortable to get to the closing in case I was deemed incapacitated by the doctor. Then I went to the doctor. Despite this accident and all that followed for me, we closed the deal successfully, on schedule, and to the client's satisfaction. We ended up not even needing any additional help or staffing.

However, on the closing call with both the buyer and sellers, and all of their various advisory teams, my partner at the big law firm called me out for "disrupting the flow of the deal." He was referring to my concussion. I think that was the fastest anyone had burst my bubble of pride until then. I was speechless. My clients, the owners, stood up for me though – they insisted that I be recognized for the unexpected dedication with which I had represented them to get to the closing, and they detailed all the ways in which I didn't let my accident affect the deal. That partner was taken aback. While we didn't work together much afterward, I was forever hooked on sell-side M&A.

I share this story as my own welcome to M&A – by the first pair of M&A clients I was responsible for – and to illustrate that selling one's company is as personal as any corporate transaction can get. I make a strong connection with each client (individual or team) that I represent in an M&A transaction because the purchase or sale of a company is a significant experience, and maybe even a personal one, for a founder selling some of the best of their life's work. Each M&A for me is a client's milestone story, where I can advise and coach them to make the most of the purchase they want to continue to build on, or the sale they had worked incredibly hard to build the value of. Founders who arrive at an M&A, I find, are often the most tenacious, resilient, and deeply intuitive in their area of specialization; and they are great company!

Often, my clients want to know me because we end up spending a lot of quality time together for the few months of their M&A. In this chapter, I share some stuff about me. I hope my story inspires you.

BACKGROUND

My journey to the realm of M&A started from the most unexpected of places – a small country in the Indian subcontinent called Bangladesh. I was born into, and raised by, a loving Muslim family in Dhaka, the capital of Bangladesh. Despite being the eldest of three daughters in a society that quite strongly favors male children, my parents invested their life's earnings into sending me and my sisters to the best English-speaking schools in the country. I graduated from the Aga Khan School, Dhaka – a foundation established in Dhaka by Prince Karim Aga Khan. During my time, the school was administered by my profoundly loving high school principal, the late Mr. George G. Kays. Mr. Kays was my first window into the world beyond Dhaka, and he created every opportunity for his students to step outside the country into the global arena. I used to debate competitively in high school, and Mr. Kays sponsored my first trip to Washington, DC, to represent Bangladesh at the World Schools Debating Championships.

Once I had seen Georgetown University and met

students from across the world who were gunning to attend college in the United States, I was committed. My parents did not want to allow me – a young, gullible teen – to travel across the world to a foreign country to attend college. I did not want to allow myself to go to school anywhere else. So, I decided to take a gap year and volunteered at a women's advocacy organization and shelter called the Bangladesh National Women Lawyers' Association (BNWLA) in Dhaka. BNWLA provides pro bono legal and rescue services to trafficked women and children, provides housing for those rescued from fates worse than death, and runs training programs to provide them with skills to re-habilitate into society. My time at BNWLA was a profound lesson in the transformative power of financial independence and economic empowerment.

I didn't have money to take the School Admission Test (SAT) exam, which was required to apply to US colleges. So, I called an uncle who had moved to the United States years ago and emotionally blackmailed him into paying for my SAT exam. If he had a chance to improve his standard of living, why shouldn't I? I also didn't have money to pay the admission application fees, so I sent out handwritten letters (my internet privileges were restricted) to colleges, requesting fee waivers due to economic hardship. Many colleges obliged. To top it off, I aced my SAT exam.

Once my parents witnessed my determination, they relented but set strict conditions. I could attend college in the United States, but I had to attend an all-women's college, on a full scholarship, in a location not far from a family friend who could keep an eye on me and help out, if needed. The rest, as they say, is history.

EDUCATION

I spent the most transformative and educational four years of my life at Mount Holyoke College in South Hadley, Massachusetts. Mount Holyoke is more than my liberal arts alma mater – it's my lifelong home and family. After graduating from Mount Holyoke with a bachelor of arts in economics and international relations, magna cum laude with honors, and as the 177th baccalaureate speaker, I went straight to a T14 law school – the New York University School of Law. At that time, foreign students didn't qualify for student loans in the United States, even private ones, without a US resident guarantor. The day before my deadline to accept my admissions offer, a family friend, Mr. Farid Khan, stepped up and agreed to be a guarantor.

At NYU Law, I was immersed in studying the laws of United States while competing with the brightest peers from across the world. I was at the top of my class during the first year and also had the honor of serving as the executive editor of the *NYU Law Review*. Had I not been able to achieve these standards of academic success, I wouldn't have qualified for a big law firm job. Through the T14 law school to AmLaw100 big law firm hiring funnel, I was able to land a summer associate position, and thereafter a job offer, from a big law firm while I was still a second-year law student.

Somewhere along the way from college to law school, I met and fell in love with a sharp young man – also from Bangladesh – who was cutting his own swath across the globe. We decided to marry and journey through life together. After graduating law school, we moved to Northern California, where I began my law practice and I still reside.

In this first part of my legal career at big law firms, I

learned from, and was trained by, some of the best corporate and M&A lawyers in the United States. I cannot thank them enough for the investment they made in me, and it is incumbent on me to give some of them a shout-out.

EMPLOYMENT

Despite my beef with big law firms for being inaccessible to founders from traditionally marginalized groups, I owe my success, career, and expertise to them.

After law school, I landed at DLA Piper LLP (US) in Palo Alto. DLA Piper is a global law firm serving some of the largest multinational corporations in the world to meet all their corporate needs. I was hired into their corporate team in Silicon Valley, and that firm and team were the best initiation I could have hoped for into the world of corporate law.

At DLA Piper, I was fortunate to work with a team of exceptional professionals who guided me through the early stages of my career. They are too many to name, but I want to particularly thank Louis Lehot, who hired me, and Brandee Diamond, Eric Chow, and Philip Tsukanov, who trained me to deliver the best-in-the-world corporate legal advice in M&As. In a field where women often find it difficult to succeed, Ms. Diamond has been trail-blazing and mentoring promising attorneys for years. Many of these experts now work at Foley & Lardner LLP. My time at DLA Piper involved rigorous training and hands-on experience in various aspects of corporate law, including incorporations, corporate governance, equity financing, debt financing, and strategic transactions.

During my tenure at DLA Piper, I was involved in numerous high-stakes transactions as a junior associate. For instance, I played a crucial role in representing Neopost, a French public company and a global leader in mail solutions, advised by Ms. Diamond, in its approximately $100 million cross-border acquisition of Parcel Pending, a US provider of innovative package management solutions. I also worked on the cross-border sale of Neopost's subsidiary Satori Software for approximately $70 million to Thompson Street Capital Partners, a provider of postal management software.

My very first deal at DLA Piper that made me realize the great power of M&A was the sale of Centric Software, a privately owned international software company in the fashion, apparel, luxury, and retail sectors, in its sale to Dassault Systèmes, led by Mr. Lehot. Mr. Lehot and his team at DLA Piper entrusted me with some of the most critical aspects of the deal, such as the stockholder solicitation (which I talk about later in this book), and I had the most eye-opening experiences. I realized how a successful company exit could build generational wealth for the founder and his entire family. Among the many phone calls I received as the attorney whose name was on the stockholder solicitation, I received a call from the founder's mother. Tearfully, she told me how proud she was of her son and how he had changed the course of life for many of his friends and family, including her, by allowing them to be a part of the company's growth and successful exit. I aim to re-create this experience for the founders I serve.

After DLA Piper, I was recruited by Fenwick & West LLP, a national powerhouse born in the heart of Silicon Valley. At Fenwick, I learned the best M&A practices, and much of my M&A experience I talk about here was acquired during my tenure at Fenwick as an associate. Fenwick is renowned for its expertise in technology M&A, and I had the privilege of working with some of the smartest, kindest, and most innovative lawyers of our time. Again, I would like to name and thank all my colleagues, but I must at least express my gratitude to Kris Withrow, Victoria Lupu, and Lynda Twomey for their patience and mentorship. I was not an easy associate to coach, but they – especially Mr. Withrow – gave me more chances than I could have ever hoped for. Mr. Withrow's mentorship often went beyond our work to lifting me up in my life in general. Mr. Withrow supervised me through the life-changing experience of becoming a mother while at Fenwick and even gave me furniture when my husband and I bought our first house. Mr. Withrow is what someone in my position would call a true ally. He gave me more chances and room to grow than I have ever encountered in big law. There are not enough words to express my gratitude to Mr. Withrow, my mentors at Fenwick, and the many incredible people I worked with there.

At Fenwick, I honed my skills by managing, and later leading, a large number of M&A deals, many of which were high profile. My first critical transaction was representing ThousandEyes, a privately held internet and cloud intelligence platform headquartered in San Francisco, in its sale to Cisco, a public networking technology company, for approximately $900 million. The deal was led by Mr. Ethan Skerry. My experience in this deal made me realize the extremely critical role that merger waterfalls play in modeling, negotiating, and finalizing an M&A deal. (I talk about merger waterfalls later in this book.)

I continued to represent companies in numerous sell-side transactions during one of the busiest M&A cycles in the US economy under the supervision of Mr. Withrow. Some other notable transactions include representing Streamlit, a private open-source technology company, in its sale to Snowflake, a public cloud computing-based data cloud company, for approximately $800 million. The founders of Streamlit are some of the most talented innovators and visionaries of our time, and I am grateful I was able to be a small part of their journey. I also represented Klara Technologies, a private healthcare messaging platform company, in its sale to ModMed, a private specialty-specific EHR systems and solutions software company, for approximately $200 million. With each transaction, I grew to learn more about M&A and its transformational power.

Largely because of the opportunity I had to work as an M&A associate at Fenwick, I had completed over thirty-five M&A transactions with total transaction value close to $3 billion when I launched my own practice.

REFLECTIONS

However, this world-class training at big law firms came at great cost to my mental, physical, and spiritual health. The learning curve for me was as steep as can be for an immigrant, nonnative English speaker who had learned how to write argumentative essays with a thesis statement in college.

When I first started practicing corporate law, I constantly felt lost. There was a significant gap between the theoretical concepts taught in law school and the high quality of legal practice I was expected to undertake right after graduating. As an immigrant to the United States, I was unfamiliar with the American corporate world in general. I didn't understand even the basics of how businesses operated in this market. Additionally, as a first-generation lawyer in my family, I had no idea about the professional service expectations of a big law job (or any other legal job, for that matter). The elite M&A industry and the big law practice are heavily guarded, welcoming only a privileged few.

Once I started at big law, my learning continued with even higher stakes. I had to continue to learn on the job and simultaneously deliver excellent work products. I had a mentor once tell me that if I wanted to continue to stay on at the big law firm and "eventually make partner," I had to work harder than I had ever worked before. He analogized it with training for a marathon and said that if there was ever a time for me to train for a marathon, it was now. I often think about that mentor's feedback and wonder to myself whether he made that comment with the knowledge and understanding of what someone from my background has to be able to accomplish in order to have that conversation with him. To me, the experience was more akin to already running a marathon for thirteen-plus years at that time, nonstop.

I will admit, I cried sometimes from the difficulty of it all in the beginning, and I am not a crier in general. As a matter of fact, crying is a common rite of passage for many first-year associates in big law and a couple of times I even cried in the company of my peers where we unburdened ourselves to each other. The big law experience is so overwhelming and stress-ful, that sometimes you cannot help but release the visceral emotions. Coming from my humble background, I was no stranger to difficulty and hard work. I welcome it. What caught me off guard really was the loneliness of being the only person experiencing what I was experiencing. Regardless, I picked myself up and carried on. After all, the job was a privi-lege and not a burden.

There is a reason why it is tough to be an associate at big law firms – they demand nothing but the best from their associates because they deliver nothing but the best for their clients. Had I not pushed myself to continue the marathon for all these years, I wouldn't be in the situation today to be able to take control of my career and serve those I want to serve.

CREDITS

I want to be very clear and emphasize that my thoughts and views in this book cannot be attributed to any law firms or employers I have worked for or to any of my clients or their representatives or affiliates – past, present, or future – or to any of my mentors or colleagues at any point in time. My views here in this book and in life are entirely my own, for better or for worse.

However, I did not want to take this important step without giving credit where it's due. I would be nothing today without the many teachers and friends who helped me along the way. The guidance, support, and mentorship I received from my colleagues at various stages of my career have been invaluable. The knowledge and insights I have gained from these interactions have profoundly influenced my practice today.

My journey through various law firms and the multitude of deals I have worked on have shaped my career and expertise in ways I never imagined. Each experience has contributed to my growth as a corporate lawyer and my understanding of M&A. As I move forward, I carry the lessons learned and the gratitude for the opportunities I had to work with some of the best in the industry.

VISION

My journey through the halls of prestigious law firms like DLA Piper and Fenwick & West has been invaluable, providing me with the expertise and experience necessary to excel in the field of corporate law and M&A. However, it also opened my eyes to the limitations and challenges faced by traditionally marginalized peoples in corporate law – women, immigrants, people of color, those who identify as LGBTQ+, and so on. Often, such peoples are underrepresented as senior attorneys or partners at big law firms; therefore, their needs are not prioritized, and they are underserved by such firms.

What is the business case for talking about this "diversity issue" in a book about M&A? Well, it's because M&A at its best is a mechanism to create value – a successful combination of companies should lead to the generation of value that is greater than the sum of its parts. As someone who can relate to underserved founders due to my own personal background, I see great potential to create value for both the US and global economies by supporting and coaching traditionally underserved founders. Even compared to other founders, the tenacity, resilience, and intelligence of traditionally underserved founders are stunningly breath-taking.

This next part of my legal career after big law is dedicated to coaching start-up founders to create value and to optimize the sale of their company so that they can access M&A as a tool for building generational wealth.

Given my own personal identities, I am particularly motivated to use my expertise to support start-up founders. These experiences and motivations have shaped my vision for my current legal practice, where I aim to create a more inclusive, flexible, and client-centered approach to corporate legal advice and services.

I advise private companies at all stages of their growth,

from formation to market, with a particular focus on corporate transactions like M&A. My practice has a three-pronged strategy to bringing big law firm–quality corporate legal advice and services to small and midsize private companies: first, smart use of technology; second, bespoke staffing; and third, flexible pricing.

Technology

Time and time again, founders I represented in technology M&A deals have told me that the practice of M&A is light-years behind in efficiency because lawyers refuse to use the latest software technology tools on the market. Many technology founders find their first M&A experience to be infuriating because much of the process still occurs on Microsoft Word documents and Microsoft Excel spreadsheets built from scratch. Law firms, and lawyers, have always been slow to adopt technology. This sluggishness is, to some extent, highly advised because the work lawyers do is highly confidential and privileged. We cannot risk jeopardizing our duty of care toward our clients by adopting any shiny technology that hits the shelves without first fully understanding and confirming through use that it is safe for the purposes of legal work. This sluggishness is also, to some extent, a result of the design of law firms, where often many partners will have to collectively agree to use a certain technology before the firm will attempt to use it.

However, with the advent of artificial intelligence (AI) and more recently the widespread adoption of large language models (LLMs), lawyers and law firms have little choice but to adopt more of this useful technology with the right bells and whistles necessary for their legal work. Start-ups recognize that and "legaltech" has become a burgeoning industry over the last five years. Additionally, taking control of my practice has allowed me to lean into experimenting with technology that could make my practice more efficient and better serve my clients in corporate transactions. I am, and have always been, an advocate for the smart use of technology to make products and services more efficient, accessible and cost effective. I am constantly looking for ways to bring M&A into the twenty-first century and lead the way in using technology to better client work and service.

Staffing

M&A is a team sport. Even in small deals, as the seller, you will likely have to engage a myriad of advisors and vendors – such as a lawyer, accountant, banker, broker – depending on the deal size and nature of the transaction. You will have to engage an M&A lawyer, who acts as the "deal maker" and who will also advise you on which other legal specialists you may need in this deal, like a transactional tax lawyer, an executive compensation and employment lawyer, an antitrust lawyer, and so on.

One of the big benefits of hiring a big law firm is that they usually have these various types of legal specialists within the same firm, making it much easier for you to staff and execute the deal from the legal end. However, if you are a small or midsize private company and your deal size is not in the hundreds of millions of dollars, working with a big law firm with many different types of specialists may be overkill and may result in a larger legal bill than you might have needed to complete the transaction successfully. This is especially true on the sell-side, where the legal work is significant and substantial, but is often reactionary because M&As are often "buyer led." Buyers have greater need for specialists and a larger deal team to conduct due diligence into the target, plan and execute post-closing integration, and take the first cut at drafting agreements for the deal. Sellers often don't undertake the foregoing tasks so they can do with a leaner team.

In my own practice as a sell-side M&A lawyer, I prefer to staff my deals with specialists and team members on an as-needed basis. I operate within multiple networks of small law firm practitioners across the country who I can call on with a click of a button if my client needs particular advice or a specific service. One such network is HeyCounsel, which is a community of solo, small, and boutique legal practitioners to gather and combine their powers. This bespoke staffing is a much more tailored and efficient approach that serves the practical realities of small and midsize private company targets in an M&A.

Pricing

Many corporate lawyers are well aware of the deep pockets of their corporate clients. Their work is excellent, and their service is routinely out-of-this world, so they don't want to offer them at lower prices when existing corporate clients are able to, and willing to, pay the higher prices. It's just good business to charge more when you can. However, my law practice is not merely a means for me to earn a living; it's a tool I use in service of principles that are close to my heart. One such principle is making corporate legal services, especially M&A, more accessible to start-up founders. I price my M&A deals differently, allowing my clients greater accessibility, visibility, and accountability for the value delivered.

TRAINING ELEPHANTS

I relish the control I have over my law practice. I can choose the clients I advocate for. I can decide how to best serve their needs without pricing floors or constraints on branding. I can maximize my own potential without external limitations. The journey to arriving at this privilege of professional control was a painstakingly laborious one, but one I would strongly recommend to anyone. It is immensely liberating and rewarding despite the great risks of failure.

As an outside advisor looking in, and knowing what I myself have been able to accomplish, I often see great potential in my clients long before they are able to realize it themselves. I will end this chapter with a story I often share with highly promising persons who are on the precipice of deciding whether they want to start their own business or take a big plunge like selling their company. I also sometimes bring up this story when a client is afraid of making big asks in a deal.

Take the case of an obedient elephant. In the Indian subcontinent, elephant trainers can make their "pet" elephant carry passengers, or grooms at lavish weddings, for pay. These elephants are often so large and mighty that there are no cages big or strong enough to lock them in. The obedient elephants just never run away – they are tied to a short, wooden stake on the ground with a thin rope. How do these trainers do it? The trainer often captures a baby elephant from the wild and ties it to the stake. Each time the baby elephant tries to run away, the trainer can recapture the baby elephant and painfully punishes it for attempting to run away. Over time, the baby elephant learns that it is unable to escape and stops trying to run away. When the baby elephant grows into a large and mighty elephant, fully capable of running away from its trainer, it still never does. This is because the trainer has been able to do more than imprison that elephant – he imprisoned the elephant's mind. Even as an adult, the elephant remembers the painful punishments and recaptures and believes it will continue to be subject to the same treatment, without realizing that it has now outgrown its trainer.

Often in life, especially when we are feeling imprisoned, we do not realize we have the might of an elephant. I want to inspire this might in the minds of my clients.

3

NAVIGATING AN M&A

Mergers and acquisitions (M&A), at its very core, is the buying and selling of companies. There are a great many varieties of corporate transactions that can fall under the umbrella of M&A. The type of M&A transaction that is right for you, your business, and your personal and professional goals depend entirely on the facts of your matter. As such, I do not go into a deep dive on the many varieties of M&A transactions in this book.

Instead, my approach is to introduce you to some prevalent, meaningful, and impactful concepts and terms that come up in discussions during most M&A transactions. As I do so, throughout the book I mention Delaware state law in connection with M&A.

WHY DELAWARE AND CALIFORNIA?

Most start-ups in the United States that intend to raise venture funding are incorporated in the state of Delaware as a corporation and subject to the Delaware General Corporation Laws (DGCL).

The combination of favorable legal conditions, a specialized court system for businesses, and supportive resources makes Delaware an attractive jurisdiction for start-ups to incorporate. Delaware law generally favors management and majority stockholders, offering extensive indemnification for corporate actions taken in the ordinary course of business and significant flexibility in corporate governance. Additionally, Delaware's legal infrastructure is highly developed, with a specialized Court of Chancery that handles corporate disputes efficiently. This court is known for its expertise in business law, which can be a significant advantage for start-ups anticipating future legal challenges like those relating to an M&A.

Given the prevalence of Delaware corporations in technology and other industries, a lot of the venture financing and start-up resources most readily available for small to midsize private companies in this economy are for Delaware corporations. For example, most investors in early-stage venture financing for start-ups choose to adopt the freely available National Venture Capital Association (NVCA) forms of agreements, or a similar variant of those, and these NVCA documents are primarily drafted for Delaware corporations.

The law of the state of incorporation governs the internal affairs of a corporation. For a corporation incorporated in

Delaware, Delaware's laws – DGCL (among others) – will govern its internal affairs. Since most start-ups are Delaware corporations, when those start-ups are partaking in an M&A, the DGCL governs how that start-up should conduct itself (corporate governance). This is why my focus in this book will be on DGCL.

However, it should go without saying that if your business is not incorporated in Delaware as a corporation, then DGCL will not apply to you. Even if DGCL does not apply to you, much of the laws and practices relating to M&A in other US states is still often influenced by Delaware case law surrounding M&A. Additionally, M&A lawyers will often choose to have Delaware contract law apply to the definitive agreement in a deal even when one or more of the constituent companies in the M&A may not be incorporated in Delaware. Therefore, much of the general guidance in this book could be applicable to any US company in any state looking to be sold or acquired.

In my neck of the woods, many start-ups that are head-quartered in California are incorporated in Delaware as corporations. These companies can face a unique corporate governance situation. During an M&A, Section 2115 of California's Corporations Code (the CCC) can subject a foreign corporation, such as a Delaware corporation, to certain California corporate governance laws if that foreign corporation is considered a "quasi-California" corporation. In general, a corporation can be considered a quasi-California corporation if more than 50 percent of its business is conducted in California and more than 50 percent of its voting securities are held by California residents. This "long arm" of the California statute is unique in imposing California's corporate governance rules on a foreign corporation during an M&A. With this in mind, I will sometimes contrast Delaware law with California law where I think such a background may be helpful for you.

The majority of my corporate clients are incorporated in Delaware, while I am licensed to practice law in California. This cross-jurisdictional is common practice for transactional lawyers in the United States. Specifically for my state, California allows lawyers licensed and in good standing in this state to represent clients, including corporations, domiciled or incorporated in another state like Delaware in various legal matters, including corporate transactions like M&A.

MERGERS AND ACQUISITIONS (M&A)

M&A is a series of one or more corporate transactions – any agreement, arrangement or activity – that, upon their completion, results in a "change of control" of one or more constituent companies in such transactions.

A change of control means a new person or entity acquires – directly or indirectly – control over another entity. Delaware law (and laws of other applicable states) provide specific requirements and protections for stockholders (and other securities holders) during such change of control transactions. The primary role of an M&A lawyer, like myself, is to advise the company on how to comply with such applicable corporate governance laws and existing contractual obligations during an M&A.

Various types of M&A transactions could lead to a change of control. While we cannot cover most of them in this book, at a very high level you should keep in mind that M&A transactions fall into three categories:

1. **Merger by Law:** Statutory merger or reorganization (under state and federal laws) of a company.
2. **Stock Sale:** Sale of at least a majority of the voting securities (like shares or units) of a company.
3. **Asset Sale:** Sale of all or substantially all of the assets of a company.

I briefly explore these three types of M&A transaction structures now to obtain a basic understanding as a foundation for our discussion on M&A. In later chapters, especially Chapter 4, I discuss the trade-offs when choosing between these different structures in greater detail.

Merger by Law

A "merger" is the most commonly known type of M&A transaction. A merger, or a consolidation, involves the combination of one or more companies (I refer to these as the constituent companies) into a completely new surviving company. In such a merger or consolidation, the surviving company inherits all the assets, liabilities, contracts, and business of its constituent companies by operation of law – which means that the parties don't have to take additional steps to make sure the assets and liabilities are transferred to the surviving company; it happens automatically with a merger. Compared to other transaction types, a merger is a neat method of combining companies and multiplying value. A successful merger is one where the valuation of the surviving company is greater than the sum of the valuations of the constituent companies. A merger can refer to many different subclassifications of statutory combinations and we discuss two of the most common ones here.

Direct Merger of Equals

Thinking simply, two companies with relatively equal value could combine directly with each other and form a new surviving company that has the combined resources of both. This type of transaction is often termed a "merger of equals." Usually in such a transaction, the stockholders for each constituent corporation in the merger will receive shares in the new surviving company and how much stock each set of stockholders receive will depend on the relative valuation of the respective constituent companies. This type of merger, therefore, has a "stock-for-stock" exchange component. Recall our definition of M&A – in a merger for equals where there is stock-for-stock exchange consideration, the transaction results in a change of control of each constituent company and therefore makes this an M&A transaction for both the constituent companies.

A relevant, real-life example of a merger of equals transaction with a stock-for-stock exchange component is the merger of C3 Inc. and Efficiency 2.0 LLC (E2.0), both start-up companies founded in 2009. C3 had significantly higher revenues compared to E2.0, with approximately $4.5 million and $15.5 million in 2010 and 2011, respectively, while E2.0 had $0.5 million and $1.5 million in the same years. This disparity led to a stock exchange ratio of between 9:1 and 10:1 in favor of C3. The proposed terms included C3 buying E2.0's stock for a total potential consideration of $45 million, paid in the form of $1 million in cash, $19 million in C3 equity securities issued at closing, and up to $25 million in C3 equity securities issued in

three earn-out tranches (referred to as the holdback shares) if
the acquired E2.0 business met specified financial goals in the
three years following the merger. The merger agreement specified that each E2.0 share would be converted into C3 holdback
shares based on a unit exchange ratio tied to the specified
financial goals, which was a point of contention between the
parties that resulted in post-closing litigation.[1] Don't despair if
this short case study raises more questions than it answers. For
now, focus on the merger by law concept and as you read
through the book, you will learn all the new concepts
mentioned here: types of deal consideration (cash of stock) in
Chapter 6, earn-outs in Chapter 7, and indemnification in
Chapter 8, that will enable to better understand M&A cases.

Reverse Triangular Merger

Another common type of merger is one where a much
larger company aims to acquire a much smaller company
through the merger. For this type of merger, the reverse triangular merger is often the structure of choice. In this form of
transaction, the larger "acquirer" company creates a
completely new, subsidiary entity that it owns 100 percent of
and this new subsidiary, often called the "merger sub," then
merges with and into the smaller "target" company and
thereby makes the target company the new wholly owned

---

1. The primary issue before the Delaware court was whether C3 breached
the merger agreement by not delivering the holdback shares to E2.0 shareholders. C3 issued an indemnification notice claiming breaches of representations
and warranties by E2.0, estimating damages at approximately $4.45 million.
E2.0 shareholders disputed this claim, arguing that the indemnification amount
was not calculated in good faith. The court found in favor of C3, determining
that the indemnification notice met the requirements set forth in the merger
agreement.

subsidiary of the acquirer. The acquirer will then pay off the stockholders of the target company in cash, stock, or a combination of both. This is a great structure for large acquirers because it does not (usually) require the acquirer to obtain consent from their stockholders and they can keep their assets and liabilities separate from that of the company they acquired, which sits as a separate subsidiary entity.

There are many mainstream examples of a reverse triangular merger. A popular one is Facebook's acquisition of WhatsApp, a private Delaware corporation, in 2014 for $19 billion ($4 billion in cash and $12 billion in Facebook shares). Facebook created the new wholly owned subsidiary Rhodium Merger Sub Inc., which merged with and into WhatsApp, making WhatsApp a wholly owned subsidiary of Facebook. The transaction in that deal was a two-step merger, with greater complexity than a single reverse triangular merger. We discuss two-step merger later in this book. This structure of a reverse triangular merger is versatile and can also be used for niche cases, like a "take private" transaction where a public company is acquired by a private buyer. Sycamore Partners Management L.P., a private equity firm based in New York, targeted The Jones Group Inc., a publicly traded retail fashion holding company, for acquisition. Sycamore executed a purchase agreement to take the company private through a reverse triangular merger, where a Sycamore-controlled acquisition vehicle merged into Jones, with Jones surviving as the new entity. This structure allowed Sycamore to pay $15 per share to Jones' stockholders using leveraged funding for the deal.

It would be a very bemusing read if I continued to explain the various merger structures in this book. It will suffice here for you to know the two most common types of merger by law – the merger of equals and the reverse triangular merger – in order to understand the rest of what I have to say in the book and to quickly understand any other types of merger structures you can encounter. Other than the merger by law, I will also discuss two other key types of transactions that fall under the M&A umbrella: stock sales and asset sales.

PRIVATE STOCK SALE

As a start-up, you may have already undertaken some form of a sale of your equity securities to raise venture funds or other investor funding. Using this same stock sale structure in an M&A transaction to effect a change of control of the company – instead of selling minority stock – is a similar, yet more comprehensive and nuanced, affair. One aspect that is similar is ensuring that the stock sale is compliant with applicable securities laws. The sale of securities of a private corporation is governed by a combination of federal and state regulations, primarily under the Securities Act of 1933, as amended (the Securities Act) and the Securities Exchange Act of 1934, as amended (the Exchange Act). These laws require that securities must be registered with the Securities and Exchange Commission (the SEC) unless an exemption applies. A common exemption is under Regulation D, which includes Rule 506, which allows issuers to raise an unlimited amount of money from accredited investors and up to thirty-five nonaccredited investors, provided certain conditions are met. Identifying the applicable exemption to be used when contemplating a private stock sale transaction structure for the M&A is a key legal decision.

In a stock sale M&A transaction, the stockholders of the target company will sell their voting stock, constituting at least 50 percent of the voting stock of the target company, directly to the party or parties that want to acquire the target company. During a stock sale, the target company remains as is and only their ownership transfers hands. This is why we switch to terms like *seller* and *buyer* of the stock – instead of constituent companies – when we discuss this type of transaction structure for an M&A. A popular type of stock sale for public company targets you may have heard of is the "tender offer." A tender offer is a public offer made by the acquiring company to purchase shares of the target company directly from its stockholders in the public market, usually at a premium over the current market price. For private companies, private stock sale for an M&A transaction is often a popular choice to get around various regulatory constraints.

An interesting application is in the cannabis M&A industry. In California, for instance, cannabis licenses are not transferrable, so M&A transactions in this space are typically structured as a sale of the stock of the licensed entity or its parent holding company. This means that instead of transferring the license directly, the ownership of the entity holding the license is transferred through the sale of its stock. However, California licensing authorities have caught on and added complex "change of ownership" rules. For example, the Bureau of Cannabis Control (BCC) – the California licensing authority with respect to distributors and retailers – provides that if there is a 100 percent ownership change, the target entity cannot continue to operate under the existing license, and the new owners must stop operation until their own license is approved, which could take several weeks or even months. Since ceasing operations even temporarily is not generally an acceptable outcome, buyers of cannabis distributors and retailers typically employ a multiphase transaction, whereby at least one of the "old" owners retains a part of their interest in the target entity (selling more than 50 percent but less than 100 percent) and remains on the existing license as a responsible party following the first closing. The BCC rules provide that if there is a partial transfer of ownership, the business can continue to operate under the existing license during a transitionary period while the acquirer applies for a new license. Once the new license is granted, the parties then complete the second closing where the remaining seller is fully divested.

ASSET SALE

Often, founders are surprised to learn that selling certain assets of a company can also be considered a change of control or M&A-type transaction.

Under the DGCL, the sale of all or substantially all of a corporation's assets typically requires approval from the board of directors and then at least a majority of the stockholders of the corporation, similar to the approvals required for a merger. This ensures that significant asset sales remain subject to stockholder oversight. The concept of "all or substantially all" has been interpreted by Delaware courts to mean assets that are (1) quantitatively vital to the operation of the corporation and (2) whose sale substantially affects the existence and purpose of the corporation. In addition to corporate governance laws, federal tax laws also come into play in determining whether an asset sale can be considered a merger (this phenomenon is referred to as a "de facto merger").

Apart from corporate law, there are tax considerations in an asset sale as well. Under Section 409A of the Internal Revenue Code of 1986, as amended (the Internal Revenue Code), a change in control event can occur if there is a sale of a "substantial portion" of a corporation's assets, defined as 40 percent or more of the total gross fair market value of all the corporation's assets. In short, start-ups can unintentionally trip up if they seek to undertake a significant asset sale without consulting with their advisors first to check whether the transaction falls into M&A territory. As you likely expect now, much of the Delaware case law for such asset sales relate to whether an asset sale would have constituted a de facto merger, where this doctrine exists to protect creditors and stockholders when statutory compliance is lacking in asset sales.

> **Throughout the book, I refer to any of these three types of change of control transactions – merger by law, like a direct merger of equals or a reverse triangular merger where a larger buyer acquires a target company; the sale of at least a majority of the private stock; or the sale of all or substantially all assets – when I refer to an "M&A."**

For consistency, this is how I use certain terms: The term *target company* means a legal entity, often a private Delaware C corporation for the purposes of this book, that is the owner of the assets sold, whose private stock is sold in a stock sale or a constituent company in a merger. The term *seller* means the seller(s) of the assets in asset sales, the selling stockholder(s) in stock sales, and the stockholders of the constituent company in a merger. The terms *seller* and *target business* are often interchangeable. The term *buyer* means the purchaser or buyer of the assets or stock, or in the case of merger transactions, the acquirer.

M&A TRANSACTION LIFECYCLE

This book aims to follow the typical linear progression of a private M&A transaction – whether it be a merger by law, a private majority stock sale, or the sale of all or substantially all assets. However, in order to make the information here useful, the concepts are not all presented in the order that they could appear to you in an M&A. So, for this part of the book, I want to give you a typical overview of the M&A lifecycle and how the chapters weave into that narrative.

Most M&A transactions have the following phases in their life cycle: the Shopping Period, Exclusivity Period, and Interim Period.

M&A transactions have the following milestones that separate these phases: the signing of the letter of intent (LOI) at the end of the Shopping Period often begins the Exclusivity Period; the signing of the definitive agreement for the M&A at the end of the Exclusivity Period locks the parties into a deal and often begins the Interim Period; and the closing of the M&A deal pursuant to the terms of the definitive agreement completes the transaction, often at the end of the Interim Period. The period after the closing of an M&A is the Post-Closing Period. The rest of this chapter describes each of these periods in an M&A's life cycle and situates the contents of this book within the M&A life cycle.

Shopping Period

The next few chapters in the book – Chapters 4 through 6 – are about the Shopping Period. The Shopping Period is exactly as it sounds – here you shop for one or more partners, vendors, and advisors to your M&A transaction. It's a lot like intentionally beginning to date eligible bachelors (all genders or nonconforming identities included) and deciding which group of your friends get to vote "hot or not" on potential partners you date.

Before you start to put yourself out there to date, you likely do an evaluation of yourself. You think about whether your current haircut or wardrobe presents you at your best to attract the most eligible bachelor that you can and if it doesn't, you invest in a makeover to get the desired look. Similarly, this is the time in the M&A life cycle where you prepare your business for sale. If you know that an M&A is in the horizon for your company, this becomes a more time-constrained exercise. Your business will be scrutinized in depth and at length by potential buyers, so you should make sure your business is as presentable as it can be. Chapter 4 of this book provides guidelines on how to prepare for an M&A.

Another aspect of the Shopping Period is to identify the type of M&A partner that you want. What type of a relationship are you looking for? Do you want to get married and live off your partner's income? Do you want to be in a more equal partnership where you continue your career after marriage, and you expect your partner to share the burden of raising a family? As you can imagine, much of the experience of finding the right partner depends on what you want out of your relationship and your partner. That experience is not much different (conceptually) from selecting an M&A partner and the transaction type you want to enter into with them.

You can identify the right M&A partner and transaction type if you have a clear understanding of what your goals are for yourself and your business. If you are completely caught off-guard with an unsolicited LOI to have your company acquired, like Sarah did in our first chapter, there are still steps you can take during the day-to-day planning, strategy, and operations of your business that can put you in a favorable position to receive and evaluate such proposals. In Chapter 5, I guide you through the process of how to identify the right buyer for your company to achieve your business goals.

The Shopping Period is also the time when you begin to engage your M&A advisors. In life, you likely have friends or family you turn to for advice when you are considering dating or marrying someone. However, for a business, this team of advisors you lean on during an M&A doesn't organically appear – you have to curate this team intentionally and deliberately. In Chapter 5, I discuss at length whether and how you should engage an investment banker to advise you on the sale of your company.

Once you are prepared to date, and you have decided you want to date someone, there is usually a conversation where the two of you decide you are now in a committed relationship. This declaration of commitment is akin to signing the LOI. The final act of the Shopping Period is the signing of the LOI with the potential M&A partner you have selected.

Most of what is set out in the LOI is not binding – which means that parties don't have to follow those terms – just like being in a committed relationship is not as binding as a marriage. Usually, the term that is binding in an LOI is the exclusivity provision – where you and the buyer commit to negotiate a deal only with each other and don't shop the transaction to anyone else. Some very important deal terms, including the top-line purchase price of your company, will be negotiated and determined during the LOI phase. Even though these LOI terms are usually not binding, they are significant to the transaction and carry moral weight. They are used as a basis to negotiate the entire M&A deal. Therefore, Chapter 6 is dedicated to negotiating the LOI. In that chapter we discuss, at a high-level, how to determine the ideal structure for your M&A transaction, and how the type of consideration used to pay the sellers or target company in an M&A affects the deal.

Tips on Hiring an M&A Lawyer

In addition to engaging an investment banker, you should also engage an M&A lawyer, ideally prior to negotiating and signing the LOI. As with any advisor, you should hire an M&A lawyer you trust. I mention here a few common pitfalls I have seen clients experience in engaging M&A lawyers and leave it at that.

First, founders often hire prestigious big law firms at a hefty price tag to signal to potential buyers that they themselves are a top-shelf business. This signaling can be important, but you should consider whether you are purchasing prestige at the cost of better legal representation. You should also consider how valuable you, your business, and your M&A transaction would be as a client to such a prestigious big law firm. Since you are in business, you know that the truth of the matter is client service can differ based on how important a client is to a vendor and such big law firm vendors operate like any other business. Especially when it comes to the practice of M&A, client service can make a big difference in your deal outcomes.

Second, founders often hire lawyers based on referrals

they receive from colleagues, friends, or family. Hiring lawyers through referrals is a great idea because you have some assurance that the lawyer will be good. However, like any other referral-based engagement, it limits the pool of candidates you would consider. Here, I would recommend that you interview multiple potential M&A lawyers that you shortlist through various means – some through referrals and others that you identify through independent research or other means.

Third and finally, it's very important to know that you can change your M&A lawyer if you don't think they are a good fit even after you start working with them. Most clients do not do this because it usually takes more time and effort to engage and on-board a new attorney once a transaction is underway. Some attorneys insist on sticky agreements to ensure their clients don't ditch them halfway. However, you can prepare for this eventuality by going through an interview and short-listing process, so you have alternatives ready to go, and by ensuring you don't tie yourself up in an engagement with a lawyer you haven't had a chance to work with. You can also use the LOI negotiating process as a test period to see if you like your M&A lawyer. If you don't, or if you want an upgrade, you can take the signed LOI to another shop.

Exclusivity Period

Once you sign an LOI and agree to exclusivity with a potential M&A partner, you have now entered the Exclusivity Period of the deal. This is very much an experience akin to being in a committed relationship, since you are now negotiating a transaction with one identified potential M&A partner. The potential buyer will now start digging into your business and trying to uncover any red flags – this is the due diligence process in full swing. Due diligence in M&A involves a comprehensive review and analysis of all applicable aspects of the target company to ensure that the acquisition is sound and to identify any potential risks or issues – legal, financial, or otherwise. A potential M&A partner will begin financial due diligence on the target company during the Shopping Period to inform their determination of the top-line purchase price they want to propose in the LOI.

After the LOI is signed, the due diligence process balloons and the potential buyer expands the focus and depth of scrutiny. If you are receiving stock as consideration in the deal or it's more of a merger of equals, then you will also have reason to conduct diligence on your M&A partner. There is so much focus and discussion on the due diligence process among most M&A practitioners that I decided to give this part short shrift in this book. However, I do describe it and address it in Chapter 4, where I introduce the concept of "self-diligence" as part of your preparation for selling your company.

The Exclusivity Period also involves the meat of the deal structuring and negotiation.

Usually the buyer's M&A lawyer will send over the first draft of the definitive agreement in the deal – the key binding agreement governing the transaction.

The definitive agreement can take various forms depending on the type of M&A transaction in question – if it's a merger, then it's usually a merger agreement; if it's a stock sale, then it's a stock purchase agreement. There is no hard and fast rule on what title your definitive agreement should have as long as your M&A lawyer is putting the advised terms in place to negotiate a good deal for you. I dedicate a number of chapters to talking about some of the most impactful terms you will negotiate in connection with the definitive agreement.

One of them is Chapter 7, where I just focus on the purchase price terms. I walk you through the flavors of purchase price terms, its adjustments, and how they can operate in a deal such that the top-line purchase price agreed to in the LOI ends up looking far off from the take-home purchase price at the closing of the transaction. My discussion of purchase price terms is in no way exhaustive because M&A lawyers are creative, and they can, and do, come up with tailored solutions to each transaction and its constraints. However, Chapter 7 is meant to give you an overview of the many flavors of purchase price terms you can encounter.

In Chapter 8, I discuss the nonpurchase price–related provisions that can affect how much risk you carry in executing the deal. I call them "risk-shifting provisions." Here I discuss what indemnification is and explore how parties structure indemnification terms to shift deal risk from the buyer to the seller. I touch briefly on the concept of fraud in connection with an M&A at the end of Chapter 8. The purpose of Chapter 8 is to introduce you to the key M&A concept of indemnification that you should know before negotiating an M&A deal. The following two chapters go deeper into risk-shifting provisions.

In Chapter 9, I provide practical guidance on how to review representations and warranties and prepare disclosures about the target business to mitigate risk when the breach of representations and warranties about the target business can be a basis for an indemnification claim by the buyer. The litigation in the C3 and E2.0 merger was brought under the indemnification provisions in that deal due to an alleged breach of representations and warranties by E2.0.

Chapter 10 discusses some important post-closing covenants that relate to post-closing employment of key executives of the target company. In Chapter 10, I discuss terms related to a party's behavior in the Post-Closing Period that are negotiated during the Exclusivity Period, and what risks they can pose to the seller. In Chapter 10, I aim to impress on you that, even while the M&A journey in practice intertwines your personal goals with your business goals, you should take the time to think of yourself as an individual employee separate from the roles you play in your business as its key executive officer or director. This distinction is particularly important to have as you negotiate the M&A deal to be favorable to both you as an individual and to your stockholders as their fiduciary.

The end of the Exclusivity Period is usually marked by the signing of the definitive agreement by the parties to the deal. Most buyers will aim to have the signed agreement in place before the exclusivity period in the LOI expires so that the target cannot walk away from the deal after they have invested substantial resources on diligence and negotiation. At the risk of straining a metaphor, I won't analogize signing the definitive agreement between you and your M&A partner to an engagement with someone you are in a committed relationship with. Signing a definitive agreement is more akin to marriage than an engagement, but really there is no good metaphorical illustration here. In essence, signing the definitive agreement means that the board of directors of the company has agreed on the terms on which they will sell the company, but the company is not sold yet. The agreement often includes one or more closing conditions that the target company or constituent companies must meet before they are ready to close the sale. This is when we enter the Interim Period – where we know both parties want to close a deal based on agreed terms, but something is getting in their way.

Sometimes, if there are no closing conditions that parties must wait on, they can sign the definitive agreement and close the deal at the same time – this is referred to as a simultaneous sign and close. However, for most companies being sold, this is not a practical option. Of the 108 deals analyzed in the 2023 ABA M&A Deal Points Study, 82 of them had a deferred closing (separate signing and closing) while only 26 closed simultaneously. The period of time between signing and closing, which could be a few days to a month or more, is referred to as the Interim Period.

Interim Period

Under the DGCL, the board of directors must first approve the M&A of the corporation. In practice this looks like one or more board meetings, depending on what is reasonable and appropriate for the transaction, where the executives and certain advisors present the status of the M&A to the board of directors and ask the board to advise on and approve milestones, like the LOI and key deal terms as they evolve. Once the board of directors has approved the deal set out in a final negotiated definitive agreement and duly authorized a specific executive – most often the CEO – that officer will then enter into the definitive agreement with the M&A partner on behalf of the corporation. That is, however, not enough.

After the board approval, the corporation often has to undertake a stockholder solicitation to obtain consent from its stockholders to the transaction. Depending on the stockholder distribution of the corporation, this could be a critical exercise necessary to obtain the required stockholder votes to consummate the deal. Under the DGCL, a majority of the outstanding stock entitled to vote must approve the M&A.

However, often preferred stockholders negotiate for themselves additional rights during their venture financing of the target company, including voting rights, in the event of a change of control transaction. So, in addition to the minimum requirements for the DGCL, a corporation has to also comply with these additional stockholder rights it has negotiated along the way. Such stockholder solicitation is often a key undertaking for a target company during the Interim Period.

If parties have met all closing conditions prior to the signing of the definitive agreement of the M&A, the parties can simultaneously sign and close the deal. In such a scenario, there is no Interim Period. However, most often there is an Interim Period, however short, because parties want to sign a deal as soon as the terms are agreed on without logistical delays.

If a deal is expected to have an Interim Period, especially a significant one, then parties have to negotiate a separate section in the definitive agreement laying out what the target company is (or is not) allowed to do during the Interim Period to ensure that the buyer receives the business at closing in the same condition as it conducted diligence on it until the signing of the definitive agreement and as the seller represented the business to be in the definitive agreement at signing. In Chapter 11, I discuss some of the common Interim Period covenants, or preclosing covenants, and provide an overview of closing conditions that must be met before a deal can close. In that discussion, I also outline some strategies for the target company to maximize the chances of closing the deal.

THE CLOSING

The closing is the completion of the M&A transaction that joins the companies together according to the terms and conditions negotiated in the definitive agreement. If it is a merger, then the closing is the act of filing a Certificate of Merger with the appropriate state government authority – for Delaware target or constituent companies this is the Delaware Secretary of State's office. Once the Certificate of Merger is certified by the company, the constituent companies are no more and there is a new surviving company. If it's a stock sale, then this is where old share certificates held by the sellers are canceled and new shares with certificates are issued to the new stockholder(s). If it's an asset sale, then this is also the time when the assets are handed over or transferred to the buyer.

Closing is also the event on which the buyer pays the deal consideration to the seller. Sometimes I encounter executives or stockholders in the target company who expect to get paid when they sign the definitive agreement or provide stockholder approval for the deal. It's a common misunderstanding. If you have a separate signing and closing in your deal, you don't get paid at signing or until the closing occurs.

The closing is akin to a marriage but without the concept of a divorce. If parties want an out, they have to contemplate and negotiate the risk of a signed deal not closing potentially. Termination fees come into play here and I discuss them in Chapter 11. Once a merger closes, the two companies are combined forever. It is not possible to reverse a merger. If a mistake is made, another M&A-type transaction must be undertaken to try to mitigate the negative effects. While the same sense of formality is not true for stock sales or asset sales, in essence they are all life-altering events for the constituent or target company. Once an M&A closes, there is no going back. Parties can only try to address any errors and issues as they move forward after the transaction.

Once you have closed the deal, you are now in the Post-Closing Period. This is where your target company integrates with the buyer's larger business or where you deal with post-closing obligations or duties you previously negotiated, depending on the nature of the transaction. However, I don't discuss the Post-Closing Period in this book because this period is of greater concern to a buyer than a seller (or target). As a seller or founder of a target company subject to an acquisition, much of the work you do until the closing of the transaction will determine what the Post-Closing Period will look like for you. I weave in post-closing discussion within the existing chapters. You won't have much control over the Post-Closing Period because now control of your company has changed to another.

FIDUCIARY DUTIES

You will notice that I did not mention Chapter 12. This is because Chapter 12 is a freestanding chapter and is also the chapter where I, out of necessity, discuss a lot of Delaware case law. For most of this book I try to maintain a narrative style without bringing in references to statutes and case law. However, a critical part of M&A is the corporate duties you have to fulfill as a director and executive of the constituent or target company. These duties during an M&A cannot be understood without my discussing with you the case law that have shaped those duties over the years. These duties are important for you to know at any stage of the M&A process from shopping to closing and beyond. However, to make it easier for you, instead of talking about case law throughout the book, I wrote a stand-alone chapter just on the rules you have to follow in an M&A. Try not to skip over it as you read the book. Even if you do skip over it, do make sure you get your M&A lawyer to explain these rules to you before you dive into the exciting world of mergers and acquisitions.

As you read through the book, keep in mind the lifecycle of the M&A: the Shopping Period, the Exclusivity Period and the Interim Period; with each successive period initiated by the milestones of signing the Letter of Intent, entering into the definitive transaction agreement at signing, and then, if there is a separate sign and close, consummating the transaction at the closing. It will be easier to understand the concepts discussed here once they are situated within this transaction lifecycle.

4

PREPARING FOR SALE

American racecar driver Bobby Unser famously said: "Success is where preparation and opportunity meet." This is true both in dating and in M&A. Particularly in M&A, the business you conduct today can create opportunities for a successful M&A in the future. In this chapter, I focus on the "preparation" aspect of success while in the next chapter, when discussing selecting a buyer, I focus more on how you can prepare to receive "opportunity" as well.

I will begin by discussing preparation tactics that you can undertake when you have already arrived at an M&A and then work backward to discussing preparation tactics you should consider undertaking at any time of your start-up life cycle to set the stage for successfully beginning and closing an M&A in the future. When you have arrived at an M&A, you are advised to conduct a "self-diligence." Self-diligence is the exercise of investigating your own company like a potential buyer would. Within self-diligence, I reveal tips on how you can add value to certain aspects of your business. I then go on to discuss how your fundraising decisions today can affect your M&A opportunities in the future. I provide insight on how particular terms in your existing organizational documents or stockholder agreements that you negotiate today can later affect your success at an M&A.

As you read through this chapter, please remember that there are no rules, or even famous guiding quotes, about how you should best prepare for an M&A – the process will be unique to you, your business, and your goals. My goal in this chapter is to present you with various tools – both offensive and defensive – to demonstrate what the process of preparing for an M&A can be like. The process can be advised and guided, but it is envisioned and led by you.

SELF-DILIGENCE BEFORE DUE DILIGENCE

I introduced you to the concept of due diligence in the previous chapter. Recall that due diligence in M&A is conducted primarily by the potential buyer, and it involves a comprehensive review and analysis of all applicable aspects of the target company to ensure that the acquisition is sound and to identify any potential risks or issues. As a founder of the target company, you will experience this due diligence process in waves.

Initially, you will undergo financial due diligence conducted by potential buyer hopefuls during the Shopping Period. Primarily, the potential buyer hopefuls want to decide whether your target company is a sound financial investment and they conduct Quality of Earnings (QofE) diligence. This involves an independent analysis of a company's financial records to verify the accuracy and sustainability of its earnings. The key aspects of QofE diligence will use your start-up's financial statements and related information (like accounting policies) to determine the top-line purchase price they want to propose in an LOI offer to purchase the company. Once you have signed an LOI and entered into an exclusive arrangement with a potential buyer, that buyer will dig in and conduct a much more comprehensive and thorough diligence process during the Exclusivity Period. This thorough due diligence will span all aspects of the business in addition to finance. As the potential buyer uncovers information about your business, it will use such information to negotiate the details of the deal and, in some extreme cases, to even revise the top-line purchase price and key purchase terms you may have agreed to in the LOI. A potential buyer could also uncover information that makes the buyer walk away from the deal entirely.

Sometimes, the deal falls through based on what is uncovered in due diligence but there is no fault of either party. This happened in one of my deals. Both parties had been engaged in a potential acquisition process for months. They had signed an LOI for a lucrative deal and were knee-deep in a very thorough due diligence process and a heated negotiation of the definitive agreement when they realized they couldn't go through with the M&A. One of the key customers for the target company was a direct competitor of the potential buyer. The target company prudently did not reveal the identities of its customers earlier in the due diligence process, even though they had a confidentiality agreement in place with the potential buyer. When the potential buyer finally learned about the identity of this key customer days away from signing the deal, they informed the target company of the pickle. The potential buyer did not want to incite retaliation from an already enraged competitor, and the target company did not want to lose an important revenue-generating account – and thereby lose value – by attempting to sell to their key customer's sworn enemy. The parties walked away from the deal.

You cannot guarantee that if you respond to the due diligence process perfectly, with adequate forethought and
preparation, that the M&A deal will successfully close. That's
the opportunity part of the equation. However, the possibility
of a missed opportunity cannot deter you from using all the
tools at your disposal from preparing for a successful M&A.

**The most impactful way in which you can
substantively prepare for an M&A – and the
due diligence onslaught from potential buyers –
is by conducting a due diligence exercise on
your target company yourself. This is the "self-
diligence" exercise.**

Recall our dating metaphor from the last chapter, where
we said preparation for M&A is akin to doing a self-evaluation
and, if necessary, getting a makeover to attract your ideal partner. Self-diligence is that self-evaluation and, if necessary,
involves getting a "makeover" for your target company. What
this process looks like for you and your business is unique to
the facts. However, for all companies, this self-diligence exercise is a meaningful departure from their day-to-day operations because self-diligence requires the company to take a
long, hard look at their own value proposition from the lens of
a prospective buyer. Often and organically, your ongoing self-
diligence process might overlap with and merge into a potential buyer's due diligence on your target company.

Self-diligence is a structured and methodical process,
often guided by an investment banker or your company's
corporate or M&A lawyer. Self-diligence can be structured in
the way a potential buyer would structure their due diligence
on your target company, but it need not be structured that
way. I advise modeling your self-diligence after a potential

buyer's due diligence process because that is the most thorough and surest way to ensure that your efforts directly flow into an M&A process.

Usually at the Exclusivity Period stage of due diligence, the M&A advisors to the potential buyer will provide one or more due diligence request lists to you, asking you to provide copious amounts of information about the target company and its business. The intensity of the due diligence scrutiny that a target company is subject to is inversely proportional to a potential buyer's risk appetite and directly proportional to its budget. Risk averse buyers with big budgets are likely to lean heavily into due diligence and send very detailed requests. However, by and large, the due diligence request list is comprehensive and lengthy, and it takes the target company time and effort to respond to it. Serial acquirers of technology companies in the Silicon Valley like Amazon, Cisco, and Meta, and large private equity buyers, are notorious for having some of the most thorough due diligence processes.

A due diligence request list is often separated by business function. Most due diligence request lists will contain sections requesting information relating to commonly found functions in any business, such as corporate organization and governance, material contracts, human resources (HR), information technology (IT) systems, real and personal property, and intellectual property (IP). The due diligence request list will also contain sections requesting information that is unique to your business and your industry. For example, if you do government contracting or subcontracting, the list will have a section asking specifically about your government contracts. When a potential buyer is preparing a due diligence request list for your target company, it is initially operating in the blind. Often, advisors for a potential buyer will send an initial due diligence request list that is standard for any business and will then follow up with subsequent rounds of supplemental due diligence request lists that are more targeted as it learns more about your business.

When conducting self-diligence, you can follow a due diligence request list that a potential buyer might use for your business. If you want a look at a sample due diligence request list that a large serial acquirer could send to a smaller target company in a technology M&A, you can access a **sample due diligence request list** at this book's website. More information on how to access the list is available at the end of the book under the heading "Gift for Reader."

You can use this list as a starting point in your self-diligence exercise. Unlike a potential buyer, you already know enough about your business functions to ask the right questions that a potential buyer should ask. You can adopt this list by removing requests relating to inapplicable business functions and adding requests relating to functions that are specific or unique to your business.

You don't have to conduct a full-blown self-diligence exercise. You can choose to focus on those areas of your business that you know require your attention or the ones that can directly affect your valuation.

How extensive your self-diligence exercise is depends entirely on you, your risk appetite, and your budget. However, unlike a potential buyer, whose investment in due diligence is a sunk cost if they later walk away from the deal, any investment you make on conducting self-diligence should increase the value of your business, even if you don't eventually sell in an M&A.

For example, if you have a technology start-up then the

scalability of your tech stack is likely a business function you should choose to self-diligence. A scalable system can handle increasing amounts of work without sacrificing on performance. Many companies pursue "buy-and-build" M&A strategies, which means they acquire strategic technology that would take too long to build internally or that their existing team lacks the expertise to build. For technology companies, scalability is particularly important. You should assess which areas of your start-up eco-system are scalable and which areas could benefit from a restructuring to improve their scalability. A potential buyer will eventually integrate your back-office systems, tech stack, supply and logistics networks, and other functions. However, they will also seek to actualize value from the acquisition as quickly as possible without making substantial investments in integrating operations, so having scalable systems that allow the potential buyer to increase the systems' workload with implementation of their post-M&A plans will make your start-up more attractive.

There are two goals to this self-diligence exercise: to identify and then to address any risks or liability.

First, during self-diligence, you want to identify any liabilities and risks, or to identify areas of the business that can be optimized for higher value. Then, once you have identified areas of interest, you want to address them by reducing or removing any liabilities, mitigating any risks, and optimizing for the highest valuation possible for your company. By definition, what you uncover in self-diligence and how you, or the board of directors at your start-up, address what is uncovered depends on the facts. Regardless, later on in this chapter, I will discuss what self-diligence identification and assessment might look like in the context of my fields of expertise, which is corporate organization and governance and the capitalization of the target company. You should rely on applicable advisors and experts to guide you through the self-diligence of the other business functions.

Before I jump into a mini self-diligence identification and assessment exercise, I want to briefly note that there is no existing standard market practice on preparing for an M&A by conducting self-diligence. Most prudent founders engage in this self-diligence exercise periodically without realizing that this is what they are doing. However, I want more founders to intentionally and consciously undertake the self-diligence exercise so that they are able to maximize the value of their start-up before engaging in an M&A process. Other than maximizing the value of your start-up, conducting self-diligence will also prepare you to logistically address due diligence requests from potential buyers and to fulfill your existing obligations.

Responding to Due Diligence

> **Your responsibility during the entire due diligence process is to grant a potential buyer access to relevant documents, contracts, and statements. Your disclosure should be comprehensive enough to allow that potential buyer to make an informed decision. Additionally, you should be reasonably responsive to due diligence requests and provide the requested information in a timely manner.**

However, you must also ensure that in making relevant

disclosures, you are remaining compliant with your existing obligations.

First, you have a duty to your stockholders to act in their best interests (more on this in Chapter 12). If a potential buyer uncovers a significant risk or liability in your business during due diligence that you were not aware of, you are immediately on the back foot in negotiations. Not only do you lose negotiation leverage, you are also now expected to address this liability issue with full visibility to the potential buyer and thereby risk affecting the deal on the table. This can raise a conflict of interest for you between striking the best deal with a potential buyer and fulfilling your duty toward your stockholders. If you conduct self-diligence, chances are you have already identified the liability and possibly determined a means to address the liability prior to a potential buyer learning about it.

Second, you may have obligations under existing contracts that are triggered during an M&A that may be of great interest to you. For example, most commercial contracts can have a clause that allows either party to terminate the contract at will. If your business has material contracts that allow for at-will termination by the counter party, you will want to know this prior to entering into an M&A where your company's valuation depends on the counter party not terminating that contract when they hear about your pending M&A. As another example, most contracts contain confidentiality provisions that prevent you from disclosing that contract, or the terms therein, to a third party. A potential buyer conducting due diligence could be considered such a third-party such that if you disclosed that contract to that potential buyer during due diligence, you would be giving the counter party to the contract basis to claim a breach of contract. If you conduct self-diligence, you will be aware of your existing contractual obligations prior to embarking on an M&A and thereby become better prepared to ensure that you are complying with these existing contractual obligations.

Third, you have a duty to keep nonpublic information confidential under applicable laws. Especially when it comes to your employees, customers, and service providers, you should redact any personally identifiable information (PII), such as a person's name, date of birth, address, or social security number, in any document that you share during due diligence with a potential buyer. You should maintain control of any virtual data room (VDR) where you share information about your business; you should control which persons are authorized to view or edit information in the VDR and, if necessary, limit their access to only specific folders in the VDR. Further, you should monitor how viewers download or share the information you provide to them, and you should close any VDRs that are not active – especially after the closing of a transaction or M&A. Also, as you likely guessed, you should enter into a confidentiality agreement with any potential buyer with whom you share non-public information in diligence. Undertaking a self-diligence process will provide you with the opportunity to appropriately set up and control the VDR and to also redact necessary infor-mation, setting you up for success when diligence hits.

CORPORATE GOVERNANCE & OTHER EXAMPLES

Of all the business functions, corporate governance is the most basic, yet critically important, function to self-diligence. This is because having the proper corporate governance docu-ments and processes is the foundation of having and operating a business, so potential buyers will expect no issues here. If any legal problems or missteps are uncovered here in diligence, a potential buyer will become critical of the business as a whole and it will give them reason to shift more risk to the target corporation or its stockholders in the M&A. As part of the deal, the target corporation will be required to provide fundamental representation and warranties – without qualifications or limitations – that the target corporation is duly organized, validly existing and in good standing in its state of incorporation; that it has all requisite corporate authority to own, lease and operate its properties and assets and carry on its business as it is being conducted; and that it has all corporate power and authority to enter into the M&A deal. (I discuss representations and warranties in greater detail in Chapter 9.)

When conducting self-diligence of the corporate governance function of your business, you can use the following portion of a sample due diligence request list as guidance.

1. A certificate of incorporation or equivalent formation document.
2. Bylaws or equivalent governing document; and
3. Board and stockholder minutes and actions by written consents (the minute book).
4. List of directors and officers (D&O) or equivalent governing persons.
5. List of D&O who are significant beneficial owners of the business.
6. A structure chart showing all of the corporation's direct and indirect subsidiaries.
7. List of jurisdictions in which it is registered or required to be registered to do business.
8. List of the permits required to operate the business as conducted.

Using such a list:

First, identify the aforementioned documents and organize them in appropriately labeled folders. Then, review the documents closely to identify any existing or potential issues. Then, if any issues are identified, decide whether to address them. If you plan on addressing said issues, determine how and when to do so.

Your corporate or M&A lawyer can assist you in identifying, organizing, reviewing, assessing, and addressing any corporate governance issues.

In my career, I have come across many types of legal issues that need rectifying in corporate governance. A common issue sometimes for a closely held private corporation is the lack of any corporate records of board and stockholder minutes or actions by written consents. Depending on the facts, this can prove to be really problematic, especially if there are no records of appropriate corporate approvals authorizing the election of officers or issuance of securities. Another common issue often encountered in software companies that provide services online and have remote employees is the lack of registration to do business in foreign states. If a Delaware corporation has substantial business connections in Connecticut due to the amount of money they earn from sales they make to customers in Connecticut or the high salaries they pay to key employees who are residents there, under Connecticut state laws that corporation may need to be registered to do business as a foreign corporation in Connecticut. Not being adequately registered in a foreign state can later lead to fines and back taxes and a potential buyer will want you to represent that the business is registered where required. If the target corporation is not incorporated in Delaware, I often discuss with the founder whether they want to transfer their domicile to Delaware during this corporate governance self-diligence phase. Recall from the previous chapter that most start-ups are incorporated in Delaware due to its clarity of corporate governance rules, which is particularly handy during an M&A.

These are just illustrative examples of the types of issues that may be uncovered if you do self-diligence in the corporate governance function. Imagine the great variety of issues you may be able to identify and address when you conduct self-diligence on all your business functions! I will share some tips on self-diligence for your finances and for human resources to further illustrate the type of value you can receive from conducting the self-diligence exercise. I will also briefly discuss cybersecurity self-diligence because cybersecurity has been in the spotlight for diligence by buyers in recent start-up acquisitions.

Finances

Often in an M&A, financial due diligence is the area that receives the most attention from a potential buyer – especially if the target corporation does not have audited financial statements. Such a potential buyer will want to review financial statements for your business for the last three to five years. If feasible, and if your potential buyer is a public company with extensive financial reporting obligations, you should plan to invest in preparing audited financial statements for your company. Audited financial statements are reviewed by an independent licensed auditor, providing a higher level of assurance that the financial information is accurate and free from material misstatements. Recall the QofE diligence we noted in Chapter 3 that occurs during the Shopping Period. Having audited financials will get you to an LOI offer from a potential buyer faster. They also reduce the risk of financial fraud and errors, giving buyers more confidence in the financial health of the target company. Zooming out to look at the bigger picture – the better your financials, the more attractive your company is in an M&A.

Human Resources

In Bain & Company's 2022 M&A Report, 38 percent of M&A practitioners cited "retention of critical talent" as the second most critical factor to M&A deal success. So, a potential buyer is also likely to conduct thorough due diligence on your human resources function and the "talent" in your company. You should assess your current employee, contractor, and service provider schedule and determine who should be a part of your confidential M&A execution strategy and how they will contribute. A potential buyer will appreciate the help with identifying and retaining top talent. Another side of the coin is loyalty to your team. Many of my clients choose to exceptionally reward their team members during an M&A as a reward for their contributions to the success of the company. This is admirable, and often fair. Some founders go so far as to assess the suitability of potential buyers based on their fit to the founder's team because they recognize that the team they assembled may be one of the most valuable aspects of their business. This is not only admirable and fair, but also an important factor that could drive toward a higher valuation.

Cybersecurity

As a start-up founder, identifying and addressing cybersecurity risks through self-diligence can preserve the value of your company and make it more attractive to potential buyers who are concerned about this risk. Most companies nowadays are subject to data breaches and therefore cybersecurity is the latest, most trendy business function that is subject to high due diligence scrutiny by potential buyers.

Nothing illustrates this better than the Marriott Hotels data breach. Marriott acquired Starwood Hotels in 2016, but Starwood's guest reservation system had been compromised in a breach since 2014. This breach exposed the personal information of 500 million guests! The breach led to significant legal fees, compliance fines, and reputational damage for Marriott. The company's stock dropped, and lawsuits were filed. Marriott failed to conduct a detailed cybersecurity audit of Starwood's networks and technology during the acquisition process. This oversight allowed the breach to go undetected and continued to affect Marriott post-acquisition.

The business functions scrutinized, and the issues identified, in self-diligence, if any, will be unique to the facts of your business. How you address them, if at all, will be constrained by the nature of your business, budget, goals, and the solutions your advisors present to you given your facts. When and for how long you conduct self-diligence is also entirely up to you and your company's board of directors or other applicable governing body.

My goal is to drive home the understanding that self-diligence can help you be prepared for an M&A by maximizing your valuation and

minimizing the risk you will undertake in selling your business.

CAPITALIZATION

An extremely valuable object of corporate self-diligence, in addition to corporate governance, is the capitalization of your corporation.

Capitalization refers to the ownership of your corporation. A capitalization table (or comparable document), colloquially referred to as a "cap table," shows the outstanding equity of your corporation and the holders of such equity.

Equity for a Delaware private corporation generally refers to the ownership interest held by the stockholders in the corporation. This ownership interest is represented by shares of stock, which confer certain rights and responsibilities upon the stockholders, and any indirect rights to acquire such stock, like options or warrants. Equity capital, which is the amount of funds raised by selling equity in a corporation, is known as "permanent capital," meaning it is intended to remain within the corporation to support its long-term growth and operations.

The deal you negotiate with your investors during an equity financing where you raise equity capital will greatly affect your experience during an M&A, when you will need the cooperation and approval of the equity holders of your corporation. In an equity financing, there are certain terms in particular that relate to a change of control of the corporation in an M&A and I will discuss tips and strategies here when it comes to negotiating some of these terms. The National Venture Capital Association (NVCA) freely provides a detailed Model Term Sheet which I encourage you to review if you are interested in learning about all the key provisions that are often negotiated in an equity financing.

During a priced equity financing round for a private corporation, venture capital investors will nearly always want to receive preferred stock as equity for the funding they provide. Common stock is the basic equity tier in a corporation represented by a common share, and preferred stock are enhanced equity tiers represented by a preferred share that contain special rights and obligations for the preferred stockholders over those of common stockholders. One of these key special rights of preferred stockholders is the "liquidation preference," which is triggered during any liquidation, change of control, or dissolution of the corporation – like an M&A.

Liquidation Preference

Liquidation preference has three tiers of preferred stock participation and investors negotiate the type of participation they want in the corporation. These tiers are:

1. **Nonparticipating preferred stock**, where the preferred stockholders are paid their due liquidation amount first and then the remainder is paid to the common stockholders.
2. **Fully participating preferred stock**, where the preferred stockholders are paid their due liquidation amount first and then the preferred stock converts to common stock and the remaining amount is paid to both preferred and

common stockholders pro rata on an as-converted basis. Preferred stock "double dips."

3. **Cap on preferred stock participation** where the preferred stockholders are paid their due liquidation amount first and then the preferred stock converts to common stock and the remaining amount is paid to both preferred and common stockholders pro rata on an as-converted basis but only until the preferred stockholders receive a previously agreed to amount called the "cap" (the amount paid to common stockholders is uncapped).

The liquidation amount itself has multiple separate points of negotiation. One point is the liquidation multiple. The liquidation amount is a multiple – 1x, 2x, 3x or some other multiple – of the original purchase price at which the preferred stockholders acquired the preferred stock and the amount of this multiple is up for negotiation.

A second point is the inclusion of dividends. The liquidation amount can, but need not, include declared and unpaid dividends for preferred stockholders. Dividends is a percentage of a company's earnings that is paid to its stockholders as their share of the profits. For early-stage start-ups, the standard market practice is to not pay dividends to its stockholders unless the board of directors determine it is prudent to do so. Often, the liquidation amount agreed to is informed by current market practices and the parties' negotiation power.

Additionally, a third point of negotiation is the granularity. A unique set of liquidation preference terms can be separately applicable to each class or series of preferred stock of the corporation. Liquidation preference provisions tend to be more granular for later rounds of equity financing since a company is closer to a potential change of control event.

When you arrive at an M&A, building your "waterfall," which shows how the purchase price gets distributed among the equity holders of your company, is a critical undertaking. We will discuss more about this waterfall in Chapter 7. Part of building this waterfall is calculating the liquidation preferences and identifying the liquidation amounts owed to your preferred stockholders in the event of a change of control. For now, I want to illustrate how important negotiating such equity financing terms can be in the event of an M&A.

Let's imagine that your start-up raised $1 million from investors in exchange for preferred stock with a 2x liquidation preference. If the start-up is then sold for $5 million, then the amount of money you will receive as a holder of common stock will vary depending on the type of liquidation preference at play. If its nonparticipating preferred stock, then the investors will be paid their $2 million first and the remaining $3 million is distributed among the common stockholders. If it's fully participating preferred stock, then the investors receive their $2 million first and then their preferred stock will convert to common stock. After conversion on a pro rata basis, if the preferred stock accounts for 30 percent of the total converted stock and the common stock accounts for 70 percent, then the investors will receive an additional $900,000 and the common stockholders will receive the remaining $2.1 million. The following chart illustrates this.

	Ownership	Nonparticipating	Fully Participating
Preferred Stock	30 percent	$2 million	$2.9 million
Common Stock	70 percent	$3 million	$2.1 million

In addition to the liquidation preference, another set of

terms negotiated during an equity financing that greatly affects an M&A are the voting rights of preferred stockholders. A certain percentage of one or more class or series of preferred stockholders, particularly the key round-leading investors, can hold a few of the following voting rights: protective provisions, blocking rights, drag along rights and right to early notice. I cover some of these terms here.

Protective Provisions

The approval of a certain percentage of the stock in a particular class or series, in addition to what is required under applicable corporate governance laws, can be necessary to approve the M&A transaction (such rights are often referred to as "protective provisions"). For example, at least 75 percent of the outstanding Series A Preferred Stock must approve an M&A transaction. More than 95 percent of venture capital deals contain such protective provisions to ensure that the start-up cannot be sold without the investors' consent. Additionally, certain key preferred stockholders can take this a step further to have blocking rights where that named stockholder's approval is required for an M&A. For example, Exemplary Venture Fund, which holds Series A Preferred Stock, must approve an M&A transaction. Even if other Series A preferred stockholders voted to approve the deal such that you have 75 percent of that series, Exemplary Venture Fund must still approve the deal. To further strengthen their voting rights, preferred stockholders that have protective provisions and blocking rights can often block the application of liquidation preference provisions during an applicable change of control event (such stockholders are referred to as the "Requisite Holders" in the NVCA agreements).

Drag Along Rights

A key negotiated term in an equity financing is "drag along rights," which allow the Requisite Holders or a certain majority of the stockholders of a corporation to force minority stockholders to approve and join the sale of the corporation under the same terms and conditions that such Requisite Holders or majority stockholders have approved. This ensures that an M&A can proceed smoothly without being blocked by minority stockholders. More than 80 percent of venture capital deals contain such drag along provisions – the remaining 20 percent is likely oversight.

Once you arrive at the self-diligence of your corporation's capitalization, the decisions you made during the latest equity financing will play a critical role in how you approach the capitalization self-diligence exercise. If you were mindful of the effect of key terms like liquidation preference and voting rights in an M&A, then the self-diligence exercise can be minimal. However, if you did not pay much attention to how your equity financing would play out during an M&A but were instead focused on the fundraising at that moment, the self-diligence exercise could be much more involved and comprehensive.

During the self-diligence of capitalization, the key focus is on assessing your equity holder base, identifying the rights and obligations of such equity holders based on the review of stockholders' agreements (or comparable documents like warrant holder agreements), and assessing whether your equity holders will cooperate with you, and support you, during an M&A.

As you are now fully aware, you will have to obtain consent from your start-up's stockholders to consummate an M&A transaction. It is highly advised that you get undesirable stockholders – the ones who demand management's time in excess of their contribution to the corporation – off your start-up's cap table before you enter into an M&A. Depending on the existing agreements in place with them, you may have to consider undertaking share buy-backs or secondary stock sale transactions. This is a delicate task, and you should engage in this exercise with caution because, if it is botched, the angered stockholder can now seek to block a future M&A or even engage in stockholder litigation if the M&A is closed despite their objections.

Securities Compliance

As a corollary to restructuring the ownership of your company to be aligned with your vision of the M&A, you should also ensure that you are compliant with securities laws and that your securities documents are in good order. One of the key areas of focus during such corporate self-diligence is conducting a "tie-out" of the cap table to ensure that all securities of your corporation – stock, options, warrant, convertible promissory notes and any other type of direct or indirect equity – have been properly issued under applicable federal and state securities laws, and that your cap table is reconciled with existing stockholder agreements and verified for accuracy. Along with your company's financial statements, the summary cap table (without identifying all equity holders by name) will be one of the very first documents that you produce for a potential buyer during the Shopping Period for high-level diligence. The cap table will greatly affect the nature of the LOI offer you receive from a potential buyer.

Quite recently in 2023, the Delaware Court of Chancery ruled on a case where the buyer had sued the seller for breach of the capitalization representation provided by the seller.[1] The capitalization representation and warranty is essentially the cap table and another fundamental representation that the buyer relies on to confirm the ownership of the target corporation. The merger agreement in that case contained such a capitalization representation concerning the owners of the private company OpticalTel. Buyers negotiated a term that required OpticalTel's cap table to be complete and accurate at the time of signing and closing of the M&A. After the merger agreement was signed, a former OpticalTel employee, Rafael Marquez, claimed an ownership interest in an OpticalTel subsidiary based on a 2004 software development agreement the company had entered into nearly two decades ago. Marquez's claim had some factual basis, which led to a dispute over the accuracy of the capitalization representation and cap table provided by OpticalTel. The court ruled in favor of the potential buyer, Antin Infrastructure Partners, allowing them to terminate the merger agreement. The key finding was that Marquez's "phantom equity" under the software agreement made the sellers' capitalization representations inaccurate, entitling the potential buyer to walk away from the deal.

If OpticalTel had taken the opportunity to conduct self-diligence, they would have likely reviewed Rafael Marquez's software development agreement, or at least identified a gap when undertaking a cap table tie-out, either or both of which

---

1. The plaintiffs were HControl Holdings LLC, OTI Fiber LLC, Rural Broadband Systems, LLC, Community Fiber LLC, and Mario M. Bustamante as the sellers' representative. The defendants were Antin Infrastructure Partners S.A.S. and OTI Parent LLC. On December 3, 2022, Antin entered into a merger agreement to acquire this group of privately held Florida broadband companies collectively referred to as "OpticalTel," which were formed by and affiliated with the individual Mario Bustamante.

could have led to identifying Marquez's potential ownership claim prior to providing the cap table representation to the potential buyer or entering into the merger agreement.

> **This case serves as a clear example of why learning about the ghosts in your closet first before attempting to sell that closet is a sound business decision.**

YOUR MENTAL STATE WITH SELF-DILIGENCE

Founders who successfully sold their company will tell you that much of the heavy lifting in preparing for an M&A is your own mental preparation. If you are prepared to enter the game of M&A, then your mental state will likely lead you to navigate and win the process with greater ease than if you are not prepared. Self-diligence is the recommended exercise that can best prepare you and your business, and therefore mentally fortify you, to undertake an M&A.

5

FINDING THE RIGHT BUYER

"If love matches are made in heaven, where are successful M&A matches made?"

Though I am unaware of the divine ordination of M&A pairings, I can share with you certain business strategies you can undertake to maximize the opportunities of finding the perfect M&A partner for your start-up. Before I dive into these strategies, I want to share the story of a successful M&A where the parties involved were one of the best matches in recent economic history.

SALESFORCE ♥ SLACK

Salesforce acquired Slack for $27 billion dollars in 2020. A study of Salesforce's successful acquisition of Slack indicates one fundamental strategy for M&A success: know thyself. Only then shall you find the one who complements you.

Salesforce is a CRM powerhouse and Slack dominates social enterprise communications. Entering 2020, Slack had lost around 40 percent of its value since it went public. After

Slack's September 2020 earnings report, the company lost 16 percent of its value, and before the Salesforce deal leaked, the company was worth only a few dollars per share more than its direct listing reference price. Slack also suffered net losses of $147.6 million during the two quarters ending July 31, 2020. At the time of the takeover, Slack's public valuation was uninspiring. However, despite this, the takeover price was a surprise. After the Salesforce deal leaked, Slack's valuation went up by around 48 percent and closed at that high valuation.

What strategies did Slack undertake such that, despite its poor performance in the stock market after going public, Slack was acquired at such a high premium? From what many M&A practitioners understand, Slack had undertaken multiple strategies that positioned it perfectly to be acquired by the right buyer – in its case, by Salesforce.

Strategic Vision Alignment

Salesforce's acquisition of Slack was driven by a shared vision of creating a "digital-first" business environment. Marc Benioff, CEO of Salesforce, emphasized that the combination of Salesforce and Slack would create the "digital HQ" for success from anywhere in the world and that the deal was a "a match made in heaven." Slack's CEO, Stewart Butterfield, felt the same way and added that "this is the most strategic combination in the history of software." This alignment in strategic vision between the leadership at Salesforce and Slack made Slack an attractive target for Salesforce.

Integration Capabilities

Salesforce's existing suite of tools, particularly its

Customer 360 platform, was a perfect match for Slack's capabilities. Slack's robust operational infrastructure and strategic goals were well-documented, making it easier for Salesforce to integrate Slack into its broader ecosystem. Recall in the previous chapter our brief discussion on the scalability of the tech stack for software target companies. This scalability advantage was in full display both for integration into Salesforce and marketability due to ease of integration with third-party apps.

Customer and Partner Ecosystem

Slack's extensive ecosystem of over 8,000 apps and integrations was a significant factor in its attractiveness. This ecosystem allowed for deep integrations with third-party applications. What really set Slack apart from the pack of potential targets was its ability to integrate with other enterprise software.

Market Position and Competitive Landscape

The acquisition was also a strategic move by Salesforce to counter Microsoft's dominance in the enterprise communication space with its Teams app. By acquiring Slack, Salesforce aimed to level the playing field and offer a robust alternative to Microsoft teams. Back in 2016, Microsoft passed on buying Slack for $8 billion and focused on Skype instead. In early 2020, Slack suffered losses after Microsoft positioned its Teams app as a competing product in the middle of the pandemic. Slack filed an antitrust complaint against Microsoft with the European Commission, claiming that the software giant was illegally bundling its work chat competitor with its Office suite. Slack's proactive litigation strategy to address competitive pressures made it attractive to Salesforce. Having a common business rival in Microsoft helped Salesforce and Slack team up to compete with it!

Digital Transformation and Remote Work

The acquisition was also influenced by the broader market trend toward digital transformation and remote work, accelerated by the COVID-19 pandemic. Salesforce and Slack together aimed to redefine the future of work by providing tools that enable productivity from anywhere.

Had Slack not had a clear vision for its own product and deep understanding of its strategic goals, neither Slack nor Salesforce could have identified strategic alignment, market positioning, or culture fit.

While the process of self-discovery as an individual may be ambiguous, clarifying the vision for your start-up in order to find the right buyer has more actionable strategies. These strategies can help you create "opportunity," which, combined with the preparation we discussed in the previous chapter, can lead you to M&A success.

In this chapter, I will discuss the benefits of intentional networking to find the right business partners – leading to the right buyer eventually. I will then discuss how beneficial the pursuit of "synergies" can be in your ordinary business activities and how that can lead to finding the right buyer. I will end the chapter with a discussion of what the economic dynamics may be like when you first engage with a potential buyer and whether it may be helpful to engage an investment banker.

NETWORKING

Your existing and future business network is an invaluable tool in helping you find the right M&A partner for your start-up.

A student of master's in business administration (MBA) at the University of Twente in the Netherlands interviewed five founders and conducted a survey of fifty-six employees working at private equity (PE) and venture capital (VC) firms in Netherlands on the processes for finding the right strategic buyer for a start-up. He found that, by and large, finding the right buyer is "a networking game." I would say this is largely true for all start-ups across the globe and well beyond the Dutch PE and VC markets, and the study validates the prevalent practical advice in the market.

The "network effects" at play during the ordinary course of business for your start-up could lead to you finding the right buyer. Your existing network of advisors – both on your board of directors and those you engage with sporadically – can be great sources that introduce you to other businesses that could potentially be a great strategic fit. If you have done the leg work in curating an effective board of directors for your company during equity financings and other investments, it is highly likely that one or more directors are experts in your industry and are checking the pulse on, or may even be serving on the board of, other companies that operate in your space. Therefore, it's critical to maintain an active and well-informed board of directors and periodically check in with them and your board to discuss whether or when to focus on M&A.

Your network of commercial partners is also a good

source. The right M&A partner can be along a business vertical – a supplier, reseller, or customer – or it can be a flat relationship with a complementary or competitive business or an existing collaborator along the horizontal axes. Slack and Salesforce had a preexisting commercial relationship prior to the acquisition. Salesforce had developed integrations with Slack to allow users to create and update Salesforce records directly within Slack. This commercial relationship allowed both parties to explore each other's culture, vision, and operations strategies and to use and explore their product offerings and synergies.

Your network of equity holders, like investors and stockholders, can also be a connector between your start-up and similarly situated businesses. Finally, your acquaintances with other start-up founders and your friends and family are potential avenues through which you can find the right M&A partner. You can also intentionally reach out to and network with people you think may assist you with finding the right M&A partner if you are aware of your goals.

As you connect with people, you need not bring up the topic of M&A for your company. The best approach is to keep an open mind – the right buyer could come from anywhere – and to remain curious about your new connection's business plans.

M&A IS MORE THAN JUST MARKET EXIT

As a CEO, CTO, or other C-suite executive, you have a number of excellent business objectives within your business plan; all successful executives do – and many of them are likely burning holes in your pockets. One way to identify the right buyer for your start-up is to ask yourself whether any of your existing business objectives can be served by an M&A or other business transaction, such as a partnership or a joint venture. Oftentimes executives may view M&As narrowly as a tool for market exit only, but it's a much broader tool than that. An M&A transaction can also involve corporate or tax reorganizations, divestitures, stock purchases or divestments, joint ventures, or any other significant corporate transaction for your business.

On a day-to-day basis, consider what your business objectives are and then consult your advisors to determine whether an M&A or an M&A-adjacent transaction can help you achieve that business objective.

There is a nonexhaustive list of business objectives that can be served by M&A. The major ones are growth, expansion, access to resources, and diversification. M&A can often assist in accelerating the growth of your start-up and scaling its operations. M&A can also help start-ups quickly expand their market presence, acquire new customers, and increase their market share. By merging with or acquiring other companies, start-ups can gain access to established distribution channels, advanced technologies, and valuable human resources, which would take much longer to develop organically. M&A can also provide access to new technologies, human resources, assets, and other resources. Technology acquirers often use M&A to acquire innovative technologies and intellectual property that can enhance their product offerings and competitive advantage. This can be especially important in fast-moving industries where having the latest advancements is crucial for staying ahead. An alternative to

IP asset acquisitions is to explore licensing and joint development arrangements. Finally, M&A can also help you enter new markets – geographic or virtual – and diversify your product lines. This can mitigate risks associated with relying on a single market or product and can open up new revenue streams and growth opportunities. An alternative to M&A deals here is to explore reseller opportunities. Whatever your business objective, there is likely an M&A or other business transaction solution.

EXPLORING BUSINESS SYNERGIES

As you seek to achieve your business objectives, you can employ the business school framework of exploring business synergies with potential M&A partners, within and outside of your existing network.

Buyers undertake this same strategy when seeking to identify potential acquisition targets.

"Synergy" is the increased revenue, decreased costs, or streamlined operations that result from an M&A.

Business executives and advisors drive to execute M&A deals when they believe there is a reasonable business case for creating a post-M&A company that is greater than the sum of the constituent companies entering into the M&A. Recall that in previous chapters I have used this as a metric to identify whether an M&A is successful or not.

A successful M&A will deliver on the business synergies that the parties expect from that proposed transaction.

There are many different types of synergies you can seek. The type of synergies that businesses seek from a transaction can depend on the nature of your business, your industry, the economic environment, and market conditions, but

the goal of all synergies is the same: the combined result is greater than the sum of the constituent parts.

In the following, I discuss three common business synergies that you can explore in achieving your business objectives through M&A and other strategic corporate transactions and provide a few additional examples.

Revenue Synergies

Revenue synergies refer to the additional revenue generated by the combined company after an M&A that exceeds the total revenue the two companies could generate separately. Revenue synergies are always a sought-after business objective regardless of the state of the economy. Start-ups can achieve revenue synergies by cross-selling products to other's customer bases, expanding into new markets and combining complementary products or services to create new offerings. Revenue synergies through M&A typically result in reduced competition within a particular industry and increased market share. Most M&A see some revenue synergies.

Microsoft Corporation's 2021 acquisition of Nuance

Communications, a provider of AI and cloud-based speech technologies, created revenue synergies in the healthcare sector by integrating healthtech solutions with cloud infrastructure. Microsoft leveraged Nuance's expertise in AI voice technologies used for telehealth documentation and other healthcare applications, integrating these technologies into existing offerings, such as Microsoft Cloud for Healthcare. The deal also streamlined healthcare solutions and clinical documentation, increasing customer adoption and generating incremental revenue. Other revenue streams materialized through cross-selling Nuance's healthcare solutions and tapping existing relationships with healthcare organizations.

Cost Synergies

This type of synergies refers to the savings in operating costs that are expected after the merger, consolidation, or combination of two companies or business units. These savings arise from the increased efficiencies of the combined or surviving company. Cost synergies are often sought during economic downturns. Start-ups can achieve cost synergies by eliminating duplicate functions and roles, consolidating operations and facilities, leveraging economies of scale in procurement and production, and integrating technology and systems to streamline processes. In a stable economy, cost synergies can still be valuable, but the focus might be more on optimizing supply chain efficiencies, improving sales and marketing channels, and leveraging research and development efforts.

One unpopular result of seeking cost synergies can be workforce reduction. In 2018, the $4 billion merger of Nine Entertainment and Fairfax aimed to create the largest media company in Australia. With this deal, Nine Entertainment and Fairfax united their operations, which allowed them to reduce headcount: reportedly, about 144 roles were made redundant, which affected ninety-two people. Additionally, they achieved a cost reduction in technology, media sales, and products. As a result, the surviving company achieved a cost synergy of about $65 million.

Financial Synergies

This third type of business synergies occur when the joining of two companies improves financial activities to a level greater than when the companies were operating as separate entities – often resulting in a lower cost of capital for the surviving company. Start-ups can achieve financial synergies by combining financial resources to improve the capital structure, leveraging tax benefits and credits, and enhancing debt capacity through more stable cash flows. For example, if a profitable start-up acquires a company with unused tax losses, it can use those losses to reduce its overall tax burden. This is because the net operating losses (NOL) of the acquired company can be used to offset the taxable income of the profitable company, resulting in lower taxes overall.

There can be many different forms of synergies apart from cost, revenue, and financial ones. A start-up can pursue marketing synergies that occur when two combined marketing initiates create a response greater than the sum of the combined response the two would have elicited alone. A start-up can also pursue management synergies by combining leadership teams to leverage diverse expertise, aligning corporate cultures and strategic goals and streamlining decision-making processes.

In Salesforce's acquisition of Slack, there were definitely

some management synergies from retaining Slack's leadership to execute on a shared vision. In seeking synergies to obtain your business objectives, whatever their nature, you will likely be led to the right M&A or business transaction partner for your start-up, and you will also be able to use these expected synergies as a metric to determine whether the M&A or transaction was successful.

WHEN YOU MEET A POTENTIAL BUYER

Imagine you are all dolled up, putting your best self forward at a singles bar, when you catch the eye of an attractive person across the dark, crowded dance floor who looks like he may be the perfect dance partner. How do you approach him? Would he find you too forward if you walked up and propositioned him? Should you just wait and make googly eyes at him until he gets the hint and walks over to make first contact? For an individual, it's hard to know. However, for a business you are looking to "date" as a potential M&A partner, the best approach is easier to surmise.

Once you find the right buyer for your start-up, you have to then approach that potential buyer to sound them out. There are many standard market practices through which you can make first contact regarding a potential business transaction. However, before you initiate contact, it would be helpful to understand a prevailing economic theory that will give you insight into what that potential buyer might be expecting. This theory relates to imperfect information. I want to lay out the general discussion here and then address how you, as the founder of a startup that could be a target company, can and should flip the script on this theory through adequate preparation.

For a potential buyer, the biggest impediment to identifying and valuing the right target company for their business needs is imperfect information about the target company.

George A. Akerlof, A. Michael Spence, and Joseph E. Stiglitz were awarded the Nobel Memorial Prize in Economic Sciences in 2001 for their pioneering work on the analysis of markets with asymmetric information. This area of study explores situations where buyers and sellers have different levels of information about the goods or services being exchanged, leading to market failures. When we apply the asymmetric information framework to M&A, buyers tend to use it to explain why it is challenging to gauge business synergies in a potential M&A and why M&As therefore tend to be unsuccessful. The fundamental problem lies in two inherent features of many M&As: the potential buyer's struggle to value the target's resources and the need for the parties involved to agree on a fair price.

Despite the depth and breadth of due diligence that buyers can, and often do, conduct, it is deemed insufficient in balancing the information asymmetry about the value of the target company. The theory goes that sellers often face difficulties in delivering adequate information about the value of their assets or business because they have "a natural incentive" to inflate their valuation and command a higher sales price. Some business professors went so far as to say that sellers have a "natural incentive to misrepresent the quality of the asset." In such a scenario, attractive deals fall through while the deals that close tend to be overpriced. In economic terms, buyers thus run the risk of "adverse selection" or ending up with a "lemon" (which is an analogy to buying a dud in the used car sales market). M&A practitioners largely believe this lemon theory to be true. Many such scholars go on to provide tips to potential buyers on how to "win" at this game of asymmetric information through aggressive due diligence, posturing, and unprofessional negotiation tactics to strong-arm a target with less leverage.

Company valuations tend to be cyclical, following the cycles of M&A activity as we discussed in our first chapter. Whenever there are periods of high target company valuation, such as 2000–2002, 2008–9, 2015–17, and most recently 2020–21, pundits proselytize that the high valuations cannibalize any return on investment for the buyers. A *Harvard Business Review* article from 2016 went so far as to claim that "M&A is a mug's game, in which typically 70%–90% of acquisitions are abysmal failures," citing the Bain & Company book, *Mastering the Merger*, which claimed that most M&As fail.

This sort of business speak puts the seller of a company on the defensive when entering the M&A arena. There is a presumption that we are out to sell a lemon and potential buyers begin with the concern that the target company is likely hiding the ball. The odds don't favor the seller.

Reading this as a lawyer who prides herself on representing amazing founders and innovative businesses on the sell-side, I am enraged. By and large start-up founders are not used car salesmen trying to sell a lemon one-off and disappear into the void. Often, the target business is the result of years and years of painstaking work, money and opportunity costs.

In my opinion, and for many of the founders I represent, selling a company in an M&A is not a finite game of a single transaction but the infinite game of human relationships.

Especially for strategic transactions, many founders choose to stay with the business after the M&A to assist the buyer with integration – like the CEO of Slack. Additionally, many founders take great pride in the business they have built and, despite prior success or failure, many dream of going on to found even more successful businesses in the future. This means they are not in the one-off con game. They intend to remain active in the industry beyond a single deal and maintain the valuable connections they make during the building and market exit of their business, including the valuable connections made with potential buyers and their advisers.

My advice to you is to prepare for the attitude that information asymmetry fosters and to control the narrative.

While the economic theory appears neat and tidy, the reality of M&A is far from it. The buyer is protected by laws that make fraud and intentional misrepresentation illegal. More on this in Chapter 8. The buyer is also protected by market practices largely developed under the premise of the lemon theory that put in place numerous contractual and commercial protections, such as a post-closing purchase price adjustment mechanism, that seeks to ensure that the buyer is minimizing any risk of overpayment. More on this in the Exclusivity Period portion of the book from Chapters 7 through 10. If the potential buyer is a much larger company than the target in question, then the buyer also has significant leverage in negotiations over the smaller target. In such a scenario the buyer also tends to have more resources to hire expert advisers who conduct eye-popping, comprehensive due diligence as we discussed in Chapter 4.

Often, it appears to me, that the target company is on the

back foot going into their first – or any subsequent – M&A while the much larger buyer has an expert army and significant prior acquisition experiences that they bring to bear on the M&A deal. In such a relationship dynamic, I find it difficult to identify a hapless buyer who can't confidently identify and value a target or its resources or protect themselves from the small eventuality that they purchased a lemon.

The asymmetric information about the target company in an M&A tends to hurt sellers more when they are unable to see an M&A deal through with the right buyer, or identify such a buyer in the first place, because the sellers are unable to convince the right buyer that the target company is not a lemon. The result of this prevailing economic theory is that the burden is on the start-up founder to convince the buyer that the risk of asymmetric information can be overcome sufficiently to enter into a successful M&A. Being prepared for due diligence and conducting self-diligence as we discussed in Chapter 4 goes a long way toward winning this argument. Also, being aware that a buyer may be spooked before the sale will help you better negotiate and close the deal.

However, there is hope. Increasingly, M&A practitioners are beginning to realize that not all M&As are doomed to fail due to asymmetric information. This is because start-up founders are not all lemon sellers, and they are getting better advice on how to navigate and win at M&A. Both the *Harvard Business Review* and Bain & Company have now begun discussing how companies have become better at M&A such that the failure rates are substantially lower now, and likely is in fact inverted. Today, close to 70 percent of mergers succeed – they now say. Even among the roughly 30 percent that were less successful, many of the deals still created some value. Bain & Company identified four major reasons for this

M&A success from the buyer's perspective: use of M&A to pursue a broader range of business strategies, more sophisticated due diligence, repeat engagements in M&A, and improved integration.

Their advice to buyers – which is equally applicable to sellers in my opinion – is that executives need to set themselves up for M&A success by curating the right team. This team of your M&A advisers will assist you in successfully negotiating and closing an M&A. One of the most expensive players that you can have on your M&A team as a start-up founder is an investment banker.

INVESTMENT BANKER

Often, engaging a well-reputed investment banker is seen as a way to signal that you are confident about your valuation and prepared to engage in an M&A.

An investment banker's primary task is to find the right buyer for your start-up and get you top dollar for it.

The investment banker can begin with a shortlist of potential buyers you hand over, or in most cases where they are hired, they will make the introduction to potential buyers as your broker or agent. As part of his services, the investment banker will also oftentimes help the target company prepare their financial statements, guide them on maximizing the company's valuation, and provide support and information for striking a good deal in the LOI.

Whether to hire an investment banker, and how, is a critical decision for you in selling your company. Here I will provide some information and present certain considerations to help guide your decision in engaging an investment banker.

Investment bankers can come in three flavors, depending on the revenue of your business, its size and complexity. This means their categorization is based on the total value of the business opportunity at hand. Business brokers are best suited to represent opportunities up to $1 million dollars. Brokers or M&A advisors are best suited to lower middle market deals of $1 million to $25 million. The expected fee structure for M&A advisors is the "double Lehman Pricing," which is a percentage of the sale but on a scale. Typically, it is 10 percent on the first million, 8 percent for the second, 6 percent on the third, 4 percent on the fourth million, and 2 percent of the balance of the purchase price. This means for a $15 million opportunity to sell your company, the M&A advisor will likely cost you around $500,000. M&A advisors often tend to be industry specific and regional. Eg, there are brokerage firms with M&A advisors that specialize in buying and selling accounting businesses.

For deals that are $25 million or above, you are likely looking at M&A firms and full-blown investment banks. This is the third category. The pricing here is around 1 to 4 percent of the transaction value and they often also add on cost reimbursements, retainers, and other fees such as a warrant on the securities of your company exercisable upon the closing of an M&A. This means for a $100 million opportunity to sell your company, the investment banker will likely cost you around $3 million. Investment bankers are FINRA certified and tend to be sophisticated professional players. Many shops, especially in Silicon Valley, contain business brokers, M&A advisors, and investment bankers under one roof and their services and pricing are on a sliding scale instead of being tiered as I present here for simplicity. In this book, I use the term *investment banker* to refer to all these three categories of advisors.

While the price tag of hiring an investment banker is hefty, the right vendor can be a boon to your M&A aspirations. Investment bankers not only help you overcome the lemon problem that I previously discussed by expertly handling cynical buyers but also bring years of deal and industry experience and add M&A expertise to your team. An investment banker will also enable you to explore all the avenues of identifying the right buyer and engaging with them – such firms typically have vast networks of business connections they can leverage on your behalf, and they have the business savvy to strategize with you on how best to maximize your valuation.

However, the challenge is in identifying the best investment banker for your M&A. If your business is a software or SaaS technology company, then you likely have a number of advisors in your industry that you can shop around with. You should interview each potential investment banker to understand the full scope of services that they will offer and to understand which one is most committed to closing a successful deal for you. If you are not in technology, then depending on the nature of your business you may not have many investment bankers operating in your industry or with the desired level of experience. In such a case, if you choose to go with an investment banker, you will likely not have much leverage in negotiating favorable terms of engagement. It is a business decision for you and your board to decide whether the cost of an investment banker is worth their services.

Over time, the private company M&A market has arrived at the perception that investment bankers often "gouge" their clients by taking an unfairly large share of the purchase price of the target company as their fees. This is especially stark when you compare investment bankers' fees to the legal fees of M&A lawyers (which are much lower, even for big law firms). However, such bankers maintain that the services they provide are invaluable for their clients.

I have negotiated some really out-there engagement terms with investment bankers. In addition to the price points previously discussed, most investment bankers will want exclusivity such that you cannot hire other bankers to also help you search for a buyer. They can also ask for hefty termination fees if the investment banker brings you a reasonable lead (where reasonable is very broadly defined) that you decide not to proceed with. Investment bankers can also demand that they remain entitled to their fees even if you end up closing an M&A deal by yourself or with another banker during a certain "tail period" after the termination of your engagement with such banker. More recently, given the advent of technology that has allowed for business networking for M&A to be less costly, some investment bankers have softened their engagement terms. However, most – including the premier shops – still aim to get the favorable terms that have been prevalent previously in a lesser-connected market.

Given the high fees and potentially high impact terms of engagement with an investment banker, you should hire an M&A lawyer to negotiate your engagement agreement with such a banker. An M&A lawyer can help you avoid some of these pitfalls in engaging an investment banker. Unfortunately, a large number of start-up founders I work with engage an M&A lawyer during the negotiation of an LOI or even after the LOI is signed. This means they have already engaged their investment banker on such banker's terms prior to seeking advice from an M&A lawyer. I hope you will not make that mistake now that you have been forewarned.

Under Delaware law, investment bankers and business

brokers involved in M&A have fiduciary duties toward their clients, which include duties of loyalty, good faith, fair dealing, and full disclosure. These duties are comparable to those of corporate directors and are limited by the scope of the agency relationship. Additionally, the contractual incentives set up in the engagement letter where the banker gets the lion's share of their fees when you close the M&A deal provide more protection for a client's pecuniary interests. The banker's incentive is to get you the highest valuation possible given their fee structure and to then get to a closing as soon as possible so they can get paid. Once the investment banker has delivered on a signed LOI with a purchase price, they often choose to push the deal to closing fast. This is not a bad thing since you also likely want the deal closed as soon as possible. However, for particularly complex transactions or unprepared target companies where it can take time to diligence and negotiate a deal, this incentive can have a material negative effect on the outcome of the transaction. If you want to optimize to negotiate the best deal possible for your company, you will have to rely on your M&A lawyer (not your investment banker) to control the reigns of negotiation with a potential buyer. This is the primary reason why I strongly recommend bringing an M&A lawyer on board early in the process to advise on your LOI for a M&A with a potential buyer before you sign it. I discuss more about negotiating the LOI in the next chapter.

WHEN YOU KNOW, YOU KNOW

Whether or not you decide to engage an investment banker is entirely a business decision for you and your board of directors. You can organically meet the right M&A partner through your network. You can organically but strategically come upon the right candidates as you seek synergies in your business through business transactions just like M&A buyers are advised to do. You can also intentionally engage an investment banker, inorganically multiply your network effects, and outsource the task of finding the right buyer to them. All of these are valid options and how many you choose to engage is up to you and your start-up's leadership.

6

NEGOTIATING THE LETTER OF
INTENT

Since we are analogizing dating with M&A, I want to share one of my favorite love stories of all time: that of Islam's Prophet Muhammad (Peace Be Upon Him) and his wife, Khadija bint Khuwaylid (May God Be Pleased with Her). It's a story where good business led to great love.

Khadija was a highly successful and respected businesswoman in Mecca, renowned for her intelligence and entrepreneurial acumen. She ran a flourishing trading enterprise; owning and operating a fleet of caravans that imported and exported goods to and from the city. The Prophet was well known in the city for his honesty, reliability, and sound judgment, so Khadija hired the Prophet to manage her trade caravans. Impressed by his integrity and leadership in business, Khadija took the unconventional step of proposing marriage through her trusted friend. It was quite unorthodox at that time for a woman to propose marriage, and Khadija was much older than the Prophet, but given Khadija's reputation and success, the Prophet agreed. Their union became one of mutual respect, love, and partnership.

In many ways, a successful business relationship in M&A

begins similarly to the Prophet and Khadija's love story. Your reputation in the market is often the first impression a potential buyer encounters. As you enter into negotiations intended to lead to an LOI, these qualities – your and your M&A team's knowledge, integrity, and professionalism – can help foster the foundation of a great business combination.

Negotiating the LOI is the first major milestone of an M&A transaction. Recall from Chapter 3 that this is akin to the declaration of being in a committed relationship with the potential buyer. Up until this point, you were preparing to sell your start-up and identifying the right buyer. Now, it's more important than ever to work with your M&A adviser(s) to ensure you are putting in place the foundations of the best deal for yourself.

This chapter aims to explain what an LOI is and give you an overview of some of the key negotiation points that often come up during an LOI, so you are better prepared the negotiate with knowledge. I will discuss the key decision points you will likely have to walk through when negotiating an LOI, starting with the binding provisions and then the most important non-binding one: the purchase price and adjustment terms.

LETTER OF INTENT (LOI)

An LOI, also called a memorandum of understanding (MOU) or term sheet, is a

negotiated document that sets out certain important, high-level terms of a proposed transaction.

There is no such thing as a standard LOI. The contents

must be customized depending on the structure of the transaction, the jurisdiction, the size and complexity of the deal, the sophistication of the parties, and many other factors unique to that transaction.

LOIs are useful to confirm that the parties have a common understanding about key transaction terms before they commit resources to draft and negotiate details in definitive agreements. The LOI is also evidence of the serious intent of the parties to get to a deal. LOIs are frequently used in complex private company transactions like joint ventures and M&As. As a start-up founder, you have likely encountered an LOI because they are commonly used in minority investments like equity financings. For an M&A, the LOIs tend to be more detailed and reflect the significant nature of the transaction.

Nonbinding

LOIs are typically nonbinding in whole (when exclusivity and confidentiality are put in separate agreements) or in part (when certain binding provisions are included).

If parties choose, an LOI can be fully binding, effectively making it a short definitive agreement. A nonbinding provision means it doesn't create a legally enforceable obligation. Under Delaware law, clear and unambiguous language in the LOI is essential to indicate whether the LOI, or certain provisions therein, are intended to be binding upon the parties. For example, stating that the LOI merely sets forth preliminary intentions of the parties, and that a binding agreement will result only afterward from the execution of a definitive agreement, helps ensure the LOI terms are nonbinding. Nonbinding terms often include transaction-specific details, such as the purchase price, which are detailed and finalized in the definitive agreement and not in the LOI.

Yet, of Significance

Even nonbinding LOI terms can influence a parties' commitment to the deal due to psychological and moral factors.

The nonbinding terms often serve as a preliminary framework that outlines the contours of a potential deal. These terms can create a psychological commitment among the parties involved, even though they are not legally binding. Certain binding provisions, such as those addressing exclusivity and confidentiality, help build trust and facilitate the sharing of nonpublic information. The moral force of nonbinding terms can create an ethical obligation to adhere to the agreed framework, encouraging good faith during negotiations. Once parties invest time and resources to agree to certain terms, though nonbinding, they are more inclined to follow through with the deal.

In my view, the LOI is a good trial round to test how the M&A experience will go, helping gauge the buyer's style, flexibility, and willingness to engage. I have seen some parties unable to agree on a nonbinding LOI and, in frustration, move on to negotiating the definitive agreement in the feeble hope that they will get to a closed deal faster. This often backfires and parties end up losing focus on the key, high-level issues. I advise my clients to get the essential terms into the LOI while maintaining the flexibility to revise during definitive agreement negotiations.

BINDING TERMS

Exclusivity, No-Shop

An "exclusivity" or "no-shop" agreement prohibits the seller from soliciting alternative bids from, or negotiating with, other potential buyers during the time period between the signing of the LOI (with the binding exclusivity provision) and the signing of the definitive agreement.

The duration of this exclusivity agreement is called the "exclusivity period." It also prevents the seller from sharing due diligence information with other potential bidders. In deals with separate signing and closing, the buyer often requires another exclusivity provision in the definitive agreement to cover the Interim Period until closing.

A buyer typically requires exclusivity to prevent the seller from using it as a stalking-horse while negotiating with others. This allows the buyer to complete due diligence without the pressure of competition. A seller may be willing to agree to exclusivity to induce the buyer to enter into the definitive agreement before exclusivity expires or use it to as a "carrot" in an auction process to boost each bidder's final offer.

As a seller, consider whether exclusivity would trigger *Revlon* duties or increased scrutiny for the directors' actions. See Chapter 12 for details on *Revlon* duties and the level of scrutiny applicable to directors of a corporation during an M&A. You should ensure your M&A team is prepared to move quickly from signing the LOI to the definitive agreement. An exclusivity agreement does not necessarily prohibit you as a seller from discussing unsolicited alternative offers internally with the board, but a Delaware court may scrutinize the timing of competing bids made shortly after exclusivity expires, suspecting discussions and initial due diligence with competing bidder during the exclusivity period.

If you want more insight into exclusivity, you can access a **sample exclusivity agreement** at this book's website. More information on how to access the list is available at the end of the book under the heading "Gift for Reader."

Confidentiality

Recall the concept and process of due diligence that I introduced in Chapter 3 and discussed in detail in Chapter 4. An inherent aspect of the buyer's due diligence is that you are sharing valuable, confidential information about you and your business with the potential buyer. Even prior to any due diligence, the moment any discussion of a potential transaction begins, the parties involved exchange information about their businesses. The parties in a deal use the information for a variety of reasons, including identifying the business synergies (discussed in Chapter 5), validating the purchase price, and integration planning.

Before exchanging any confidential information, I strongly advise parties to enter into confidentiality agreements (also known as non-disclosure agreements or NDAs). Such agreements prohibit the disclosure or misuse of confidential information that parties exchange during the diligence and negotiation of the M&A. The parties should sign a confidentiality agreement early in the transaction process, before they start exchanging information. When they arrive at the LOI stage, parties should incorporate the confidentiality agreement within the binding terms of the LOI.

If you want to take a look at a sample confidentiality agreement, you can access a **sample confidentiality agreement** at this book's website. More information on how to access the list is available at the end of the book under the heading "Gift for Reader."

Next, we move on to the important nonbinding terms in an LOI, starting with the general deal structures and type of consideration in this chapter and then the purchase price in the next.

DEAL STRUCTURES

When negotiating the LOI, one of the key items of the M&A that is determined and agreed on is the deal structure. Previously, in Chapter 3, we introduced you to the three general types of change of control transactions in an M&A – merger (by law), private stock sale, and asset sale. We provided a description of each of these three structures and demonstrated how they can lead to a change of control.

> **At this LOI stage, parties have to determine which of these three types of transactions are most suitable to the parties' needs and the deal at large.**

In addition to this, parties often choose to customize their chosen transaction type to best fit the bill. In this chapter, I will compare and contrast these three types of transactions and discuss when they are often employed. Given the great variety of customizations that are possible to these three types of change of control transactions, I will be unable to provide a preview to all the complexities that could arise when adopting a type of transaction to a deal. However, I will provide an illustrative example of a two-step tax deferred merger structure to demonstrate how a deal structure could be set up that provides tax and other benefits to the parties. The aim of this discussion is to provide you with a foundational understanding of these three types of change of control transactions so that you are able to make a more informed discussion with your legal advisors on which deal structure might be best for your transaction.

Asset Sale

Contrary to popular belief, an asset sale is often the most complex, time-consuming, and taxable of the three general types of change of control transactions.

Each asset and liability must be transferred individually, including each IP, contracts, licenses and government authorizations. The seller often winds down the business after the sale, which can be complicated. This structure allows buyers to cherry-pick desired assets and avoid detachable unwanted liabilities, leaving the seller holding the bag for the rest. As a result, buyers favor the asset sale deal structure. Sellers who do not hire or heed an M&A lawyer prior to negotiating the LOI, possibly because their business is not performing well, often come to us with an asset sale structure agreed to in the LOI because the buyer pressed for it.

A sale of substantial assets of a corporation can pose risks to creditors and stockholders, such as resulting in the inability to pay back creditors or reducing the value of the selling corporation without stockholder approval. As a result, under very narrow circumstances, a Delaware court can find that a sale of substantial assets not intended to be a change of control transaction is in fact a "de facto merger" requiring application of change of control rules.

Mandiant sold its FireEye products business, including the FireEye name, to a consortium led by Symphony Technology Group (STG) for $1.2 billion in an all-cash asset sale transaction in 2021.[1] At the time of the sale, the Mandiant team did not treat the asset sale as a change of control transaction, so it did not obtain stockholder approval. A stockholder of Mandiant, Michelle Altieri, sued the company, claiming that Mandiant had sold its "crown jewel" without stockholder approval required under the DGCL for the sale of all or substantially all assets of a corporation. The Delaware court applied the two-part quantitative and qualitative test I shared with you in Chapter 3. The court found that, quantitatively, the asset sale represented no more than 38.2 percent of the corporation's total assets, which did not meet the threshold of at least 50 percent required to be considered "all or substantially all" of the assets. The court also found that, qualitatively, the asset sale did not "strike at the heart of the corporate existence and purpose" by fundamentally altering the corporation's business. Mandiant won that stockholder litigation. Generally, Delaware courts are unwilling to stretch the application of the de factor merger doctrine , you should consult with an M&A lawyer to ensure compliance with legal requirements in the sale of substantial assets of your start-up to minimize the risk of stockholder litigation like Mandiant's.

Buyers can also favor the asset sale structure because it's often the most tax favorable for them. However, sellers, unless they are a pass-through entity like a limited liability company

---

1. Mandiant Inc. was originally formed to provide incident response services for data security breaches. It merged with FireEye Inc. in 2013, and the combined entity initially took the FireEye name but later reverted to Mandiant.

(LLC) or S corporation, face double taxation – corporate tax at the company level when they receive the proceeds from the sale of the assets and then income tax at the individual level when they distribute the sale proceeds to the seller's stockholders as dividend payments (to actually get the proceeds from the sale into their pockets). Sales tax may also apply to equipment sold.

However, this two-step tax structure may not be as bleak as it used to be in light of the lower corporate taxes recently enacted. The Tax Cuts and Jobs Act of 2017 reduced the corporate tax rate to 21 percent, easing the tax burden compared to the previous 35 percent. Though some states, like California, still impose an additional entity-level tax of 2.5 percent on S corporations, eroding some of the benefit. If the asset is sold at a loss, corporate level tax becomes irrelevant.

As a seller, avoid asset sales if possible unless you plan to incur a loss. Though buyers tempt sellers to agree to this structure as the fastest way to close a deal, it often drags out longer for sellers as they settle liabilities and wind down the business. Be cautious and deliberate before agreeing to this structure.

Private Stock Sale

Compared to an asset sale, selling private stock as a change of control mechanism is typically more efficient.

It avoids the need to renew contracts, rehire employees, or divide assets and liabilities. However, a private stock sale can still be complex and must comply with federal and state securities laws, as noted in Chapter 3.

One key benefit of a private stock sale is that it doesn't require board or stockholder consent – it's simply the sale of stock by stockholders for the buyer's offer. There are no statutory consent, notice requirements, or dissenters' rights for stockholders as we later discuss for mergers – those who wish to sell may sell, and those who wish not to sell, may not sell. Buyers who want 100 percent of the ownership of the target company may be unwilling to deal with a large number of stockholders or with any stockholder who refuses to sell. If there are many stockholders, the process can become complicated as each stockholder must agree to sell, increasing the risk of holdouts and delays. As a founder, you should only agree to this structure if you can ensure all stockholders are on board with the deal.

Tax treatment is another advantage for sellers in this structure. A stock sale can result in capital gain or loss depending on the basis in their stock. If the stock has been held since purchase for the proper period of time (currently one year), then the capital gain would be a long-term capital gain, which is currently taxed at a lower rate than ordinary income. Additionally, the specific tax benefits available for a deal structure often depends on the company's tax classification. For example, if the seller is an S corporation, then the parties to the asset sale may jointly make an election to treat the acquisition as an asset sale for federal income tax purposes by making an election under Section 338(h)(10) of the Internal Revenue Code. The election lets the transaction be treated as an asset sale for tax purposes, while still maintaining the structure of a stock sale for corporate law purposes. The buyer benefits from the step-up in the basis of the acquired assets. This allows the buyer to depreciate or amortize the assets based on their fair market value, providing potential tax savings. The seller is treated as if it sold its assets directly, which typically results in the double taxation we previously spoke of. However, in the case of an S corporation, there is only one level of tax generally applicable at the individual stockholder level.

Selling a company through a private stock sale puts the buyer in direct negotiations with the stockholders, who would otherwise rely on the board of directors of the company to negotiate a change of control transaction. Under Delaware law, the board of directors – which may include you as a founder director – may not be passive but should be involved in the negotiation at least for the protection of minority stockholders. The board of directors is nevertheless still required to monitor its officers and advisors in a sale process and any disloyalty or lack of due care is attributable to the board and can raise a material issue of whether the board discharged its duties properly under *Revlon*. I discuss these fiduciary duties – and the *Revlon* duties – during an M&A in greater detail in Chapter 12.

Mergers

As discussed in Chapter 3, mergers combine the target company with the buyer or its subsidiary using a prescribed corporate statute. Unlike private stock or asset sales, mergers require corporate action and are subject to statutory requirements. In a merger, all rights and obligations of both of the constituent companies survive in the successor entity, so the buyer typically demands detailed disclosure of the target's condition. If seller stockholders receive stock in the buyer, the buyer could also be required to make disclosures relating to the value of the stock.

Choosing a merger structure is a complex and detailed exercise beyond the preliminary decision of whether to use the three general types of change of control transactions – asset sale, private stock sale, or merger. There are many varieties of mergers, including direct, reverse triangular, forward triangular, short-form, and two-step. Apart from the variety, merger structures allow conversion of the target company stock into various forms of consideration, such as cash, buyer stock, promissory notes or earn-outs. Mergers are also an available option for different types of business entities, including both foreign and domestic same-entity or different-entity mergers. This allows "cross-species" combinations like merger of a C corporation and a limited liability company. Some states are more restrictive than others regarding the combinations possible by merger, making it essential to check the applicable statutes.

A major advantage of mergers is that the buyer gains control of the target at closing without needing unanimous stockholder approval.

The statutory minimum stockholder vote needed under the DGCL to approve a merger is 50 percent.

However, instead of approving a merger, stockholders of the target company can "dissent" under law and might even file a stockholder litigation against the target or surviving company and its board.

Appraisal rights, also known as dissenters' rights in some corporate statutes, give a stockholder the right to be paid a "fair value" amount in cash that might differ from the consideration paid to the stockholder in the transaction.

We discuss stockholder litigation in M&A and dissenters' rights in greater detail in Chapter 11. In such a scenario, the buyer has to deal with the dissenters exercising their dissenters' rights in post-closing proceedings, but those do not affect the buyer's control of the entity post-closing or the amount of consideration the buyer agreed to pay. Often parties negotiate that the cost of dealing with stockholders exercising dissenters' rights are going to be borne by the target company under the indemnification provisions of the definitive agreement. We discuss indemnification provisions in detail in Chapter 8.

The specific structure of a merger dictates its tax treatment. Forward and forward triangular mergers are generally treated as asset sales, while reverse triangular mergers are generally treated as stock sales.

Depending on the structure, a series of mergers and transactions can be considered taxable or "tax free" reorganizations.

Two-Step Merger

Mergers can be structured in one or two steps. In a two-step merger, the buyer first purchases a portion (ideally a majority) of the target's stock, usually through a tender offer to the selling stockholders directly. In the second step, the buyer merges its newly created, wholly owned subsidiary – the merger sub – with the target (or vice versa), as the new majority stockholder of the target company (either after a stockholder vote or through a filing under applicable state law, depending on how much stock the buyer acquired in the first step). This approach allows the buyer to sometimes gain control without a stockholder vote, as the tender offer in the first step secures the necessary shares to change control. If the buyer acquires 90 percent or more of the target's stock in the tender offer, a short-form merger (also known as a parent-subsidiary merger) can be used to complete the merger without further stockholder approval.

In some states acquiring 90 percent of the stock in the first step tender offer will be critical to effecting the second step of the merger. California requires that a controlling stockholder holding between 50 percent and 90 percent of a target's stock obtain the approval of all outstanding shares (a unanimity requirement) to effect a merger into a controlled subsidiary. Failing the unanimity requirement, the controlling stock-holder can privately negotiate to purchase sufficient shares to reach the 90 percent threshold to effect a short-form merger or can elect a "fairness hearing" process with the California Department of Business Oversight and seek a state permit to effect the second step of the merger to merge out (sometimes called a "squeeze out") of the remaining minority stockhold-ers. A fairness hearing can serve a second purpose as well. In a transaction in which the buyer is issuing securities, a fairness hearing can provide a federal securities law exemption from registration under Section 3(a)(10) of the Securities Act. The California fairness hearing would also satisfy the require-ments of the California securities laws for issuing the securi-ties in the transaction.

The choice of merger structure is influenced by tax conse-quences, liability, and the type of consideration—whether cash or stock—paid by the buyer. Stock deals, especially those involving public company shares, offer a range of tax-advan-taged options for the seller. In the next section, I discuss the different types of consideration.

TYPES OF CONSIDERATION

The primary forms of consideration are (1) cash; (2) stock of the buyer (or another entity), which could be public or private stock; and (3) a combination of cash and stock. You have already been introduced to these consideration types, especially the combination of cash and stock, when we explored the various deal structures that you could consider for an M&A transaction earlier in this chapter. The consideration may also include lesser used forms, such as promissory notes issued by the buyer to the seller (also known as seller financing), forgiveness of or assumption of liabilities of the target company, or other assets like gold. The negotiated LOI often includes the consideration description in its purchase price provisions.

Cash

Cash consideration is appealing because of its simplicity and because cash gives the seller immediate liquidity. This liquidity, however, will result in immediate tax on the seller. Often, sellers will use a portion of the cash received as consideration to pay the taxes.

Stock

Instead of cash, a buyer can issue its own stock (or any other equity security it has authority to issue) as the consideration.

The definitive agreement will specify the number of buyer shares that will be issued to the seller as consideration for each share of seller stock, known as the "exchange ratio."

An exchange ratio can be fixed or expressed as a formula that will yield a final number at the closing of the transaction or at the time such stock is issued. Historically, most public stock-for-stock mergers have provided for a fixed exchange ratio. Floating exchange ratios are prevalent in mixed cash/stock transactions primarily to increase the likelihood of equality of value between the cash and stock components of the merger consideration.

Payment of the consideration in stock raises numerous issues that are not present with cash consideration, including valuation and compliance with state corporate statutes and state and federal securities laws. The issues raised by stock consideration will vary depending on whether the issuer is a public or private company.

Listed securities issued by a public company will be more liquid and easier to value than the stock of a private company.

Listed securities can be valued in one of two ways: (1) at its market price on a specific date, often the date of signing the merger agreement or the closing date of the M&A, or (2) using an average market price over a specified time period. Unlike cash, however, the value of publicly traded stock is likely to fluctuate during the pre-closing period. Any downward fluctuation will negatively affect the value that the seller expects to receive, while an upward fluctuation will increase the value from what the buyer expected to pay. As a result, the parties may agree upon mechanisms to limit the risks arising from fluctuation in the market price, such as floating exchange ratios and caps and collars to adjust the number of shares payable to the seller.

The stock issued as consideration will either have to be registered under the Securities Act or exempt from registration pursuant to an applicable exemption. Public company mergers will almost always require stock issued as merger consideration to be registered due to the large number of stockholders of public companies. If the issuance of the stock paid as consideration will be registered, then the definitive agreement should contain a provision obligating the buyer to file a registration statement. Sellers should note that registration under the Securities Act, can be a time-consuming process, requiring a minimum of four to six weeks but usually much longer.

Unregistered securities issued as consideration will be "restricted stock." Restricted stock cannot be freely sold in the public market unless it meets certain criteria set forth in Rule 144 of the Securities Act.

Specifically, Rule 144 may require that restricted securities be held for a minimum of six months (if the issuer is a public company) to one year (if the issuer is a private company) before they can be publicly sold. The issuer may agree to provide "registration rights" for restricted stock, which would obligate the issuer to register the resale of the shares issued as consideration under the Securities Act. These rights can be set forth in the merger agreement or in a separate registration rights agreement between the issuer and seller.

In addition to federal securities law issues, stock paid in

an M&A transaction may also trigger stockholder vote requirements under state corporate law and stock exchange rules. For instance, if the buyer does not have enough authorized and unissued shares or treasury shares to issue to the seller in the transaction, then the buyer will need to amend its charter to increase the number of authorized shares. Such amendment of the buyer's charter will require stockholder approval. Also, if the buyer is issuing more than 20 percent of its outstanding stock (by number of shares or voting power) to pay the seller as consideration, and its stock is listed on the New York Stock Exchange, NASDAQ, or other stock exchange, applicable rules of the exchange may require that a majority of the buyer's stockholders approve the issuance of additional shares.

In addition to the valuation of the stock consideration and its compliance with securities laws, it is also important for you to understand how receiving stock consideration can affect your cash flow and tax obligations now and in the future before agreeing to receive stock in a deal. Depending on the terms of the stock consideration, you may be required to pay taxes today on the stock that you receive. You don't want to end up in a situation where so much of the consideration is tied up in illiquid stock that you will have to pay cash out of your own pocket to cover the taxes incurred in receiving that merger consideration.

Whether parties to an M&A decide to have a mixed cash-stock consideration depends on a number of factors, including the buyer's access to funds, the seller's desire for immediate liquidity, corporate law considerations like stockholder vote requirements, and tax considerations.

For example, if the buyer is a listed company issuing stock, and it wants to avoid having a stockholder vote, it may add a cash component to the consideration and reduce the amount of stock issued to less than 20 percent of its outstanding stock. By doing so, stock exchange rules that would require a stockholder vote on the buyer's side will not apply. On the other hand, if the parties want to structure the transaction as a tax-free reorganization, the proportion of cash to stock will have to be limited per the Internal Revenue Code and other applicable tax regulations as we discussed in the previous chapter. Parties and their advisors on both sides of the M&A weigh the various legal and financial factors at play in the transaction to determine whether the consideration should be a mix of cash and stock and, if so, what the proper proportion should be.

TAX DEFERRED TRANSACTIONS

Under Section 368 of the Internal Revenue Code, mergers of corporations offer about five basic structures by which the buyer can deliver tax deferred consideration to the target stockholders in stock-for-stock or part stock-for-stock for transactions (where stock is equal to or greater than 40 percent of the consideration). These transactions are often referred to as "tax free" but are really "tax deferred," meaning that there is no tax on the stock consideration at closing, but when the target stockholder ultimately sells that stock, there would be a recognition event of gain or loss for tax purposes. Cash transactions or the component of cash in a transaction with both stock and cash consideration is always taxable in the tax year received, and under certain tax doctrines may be deemed received even if the cash is paid later, so careful tax planning is essential in any merger transaction. Private mergers generally are structured as taxable transactions for business reasons, unless the buyer (or its affiliate) is a public company. One business reason is that there generally is no market for the stock of private companies, so sellers are often not willing to accept it as merger consideration.

One type of this tax-deferred merger structure under the Internal Revenue Code is a nonrecognition stock-for-stock acquisition, also known as a "B reorganization." In a reorganization, the purchasing or acquiring corporation uses only voting stock to acquire the controlling interest of another corporation. The acquirer exchanges its voting common and/or qualified preferred stock for control of the target company. Control is ownership of 80 percent of the vote and value of the target company's stock.

A Two-Step Tax-Deferred Merger

SentinelOne announced its acquisition of Attivo Networks in March 2022 for a total purchase price of $616.5 million in both cash and stock consideration. This acquisition allows SentinelOne to extend its AI-powered prevention, detection, and response capabilities to identity-based threats. It enhances SentinelOne's Singularity XDR platform by incorporating identity security, which is crucial for enterprise zero trust adoption.

Both the companies were Delaware corporations and chose to structure the transaction as a two-step tax deferred merger. In the two-step merger process, the first step of the merger was for the newly formed, wholly owned first merger sub of SentinelOne, a Delaware corporation, merging with and into Attivo Networks with Attivo Networks surviving the first merger as the wholly owned subsidiary of SentinelOne. Then, on the following business day, the second step of the merger was for the surviving corporation of the first merger to merge with and into a second merger sub of SentinelOne, a Delaware limited liability company, that was also newly formed and wholly owned by SentinelOne, with this second merger sub surviving the second merger as an LLC.

At the effective time of the first merger, all of the capital stock of Attivo Networks ceased to exist upon the right to receive its applicable merger consideration. Each share of capital stock of Attivo held by accredited stockholders converted into the right to receive an amount of cash and SentinelOne's common stock. Each share of capital stock of Attivo held by unaccredited stockholders converted into the right to receive the same total value paid to each capital stock held by accredited stockholders but in cash only. Essentially, these unaccredited investors were being "cashed out."[2]

As a result, at the effective time of the second merger, SentinelOne was the sole stockholder of the surviving corporation of the first merger and could authorize the merger of that surviving company into its second merger sub. During this second merger, each share of the surviving corporation of the first merger converted into one unit of common stock for the surviving company. With this deal structure in place, the parties intended for the transaction to qualify as a reorganization under Section 368 of the Internal Revenue Code and defer tax payment on the transaction.

This case study is an illustration of how the determination

---

2. Each share of capital stock of specified accredited stockholders continuing to provide services to the surviving company as specifically identified and listed by the parties can "roll over" their capital stock into the cap table of SentinelOne using an exchange ratio for exchange of Attivo's shares for SentinelOne's shares depending on their relative share prices; while each share of capital stock of accredited investors not specified in the short-list will also be cashed out. Other than the capital stock of Attivo Networks, all other securities were also paid from the merger consideration according to the waterfall of that particular transaction.

of the correct deal structure can be beneficial to the parties in an M&A transaction. This important determination is often made by the parties through diligence and negotiation during the end of the Shopping Period at the LOI stage. Details of the deal structure may be fine-tuned during the definitive agreement negotiation.

It is important to consult with an M&A lawyer to ensure that you are deciding upon an advantageous deal structure for yourself given the constraints of the deal.

You have also now realized that a key aspect of determining the correct deal structure for your particular transaction and those parties' business objectives depends on the tax consequences that the parties are likely to experience as a result of the deal structure. Depending on the deal size and complexity, your M&A lawyer may bring in a transactional tax specialist at this stage to advise on the appropriate deal structure for your transaction. A transactional tax specialist can be your accountant or another lawyer who specializes in this area of tax law for M&A transactions.

ENDING TO START WITH THE PURCHASE PRICE

I want to recap what we discussed in this chapter so far. We discussed that LOIs are term-sheet-like documents for an M&A transaction that contain certain binding provisions like exclusivity and confidentiality but, by and large, contain key nonbinding terms of the deal. One of the most important key nonbinding terms that the parties aim to finalize in the LOI is the deal structure they will use to execute the transaction – whether it's an asset sale, a private stock sale or a merger, and if it is a merger, what unique merger structure it is. Another key nonbinding term of the deal that the parties often negotiate at the LOI stage is the purchase price of the company. The next chapter is all about the purchase price of a private company – the what, the how, and the when of it – and I am excited to delve into that with you! As in actual M&A deals, our discussion of the purchase price begins at the LOI stage, but the details continue to be negotiated and fleshed out during the negotiation of the main definitive agreement, such as the merger agreement.

7

BREAKING DOWN THE PURCHASE PRICE

A side from determining the correct transaction structure for the M&A, the parties negotiating an LOI also negotiate and agree upon the purchase price of the target company.

The purchase price of the target company is based upon the fair market value of the target company, usually represented in US dollars for US companies.

The purchase price consists of one or more types of consideration, like cash and stock, that we discussed in the previous chapter. Let's follow the example of Start-Up Inc., a privately held Delaware C corporation whose purchase price is being negotiated at the LOI stage. Start-Up's fair market value is determined to be $50 million. The economy is seller favorable and multiple buyers are interested in purchasing it. The highest bidder offered in the LOI a purchase price $100 million, which is a 2x multiple of the company valuation. The bidder also offered to pay this purchase price with mixed consideration where 60 percent will be paid in cash and 40 percent will be issued in the publicly traded stock of the buyer's parent company. So, $60 million to be paid in cash and $40 million worth of the buyer's public parent company stock to be issued as consideration. The stock consideration will be the total number of buyer's public parent company stock that $40 million can buy at a specified price per share.

When negotiating the purchase price, the parties often also discuss any important payment terms, such as whether the payment of a portion of the purchase price is conditional and whether any portion of the purchase price should be withheld at closing. They also agree on different times at which parts of the purchase price may be paid to the sellers. Continuing our example, the parties could negotiate that 20 percent of the purchase price be withheld at the closing of the transaction and placed in a third-party escrow account for three years to serve as security for the buyers to cover specified losses arising from the transaction (more on this in Chapter 8); so $80 million of the purchase price is paid to the sellers at closing, but $20 million is placed in escrow.

The parties could also negotiate to continue to apply the 60 percent and 40 percent cash-to-stock distribution on the purchase price at closing and also on the distribution of the remaining uncontested escrow amount three years later: $12 million in cash may be placed in a third-party escrow account and $8 million worth of buyer's public parent company stock may be withheld, to be paid out and issued respectively after three years depending on any indemnification claims by the indemnified party, the buyer.

Conceptually, I refer to the $100 million in this example as the "top-line" purchase price, and the $80 million as the "take-home" purchase price for the target company at closing, with contingent payment of $20 million three years after closing. As a result of our fact pattern, the sellers are paid $48 million in cash and issued the equivalent of $32 million of the buyer's public parent company stock at the closing of the M&A. The following is a chart illustrating the calculations discussed in this example.

Company Valuation	$50 million
Multiplier	2x
Top-Line Purchase Price	$100 million
Cash Consideration	$60 million
Stock Consideration Value	$40 million
Buyer's Public Parent Company Stock Price Per Share	$10
(Buyer's Public Parent Company) Stock Consideration	4 million
Escrow Amount	$20 million
Cash Escrow Amount	$12 million
Escrow Shares Value	$8 million
Escrow Shares	800,000
Take-Home Purchase Price at Closing	$80 million
Cash Consideration Paid at Closing	$48 million
Shares Issued at Closing	3.2 million

At this stage, the parties will always make the purchase price terms – however detailed or sparse – subject to additional due diligence of the target company by the buyer. The actual agreed-on purchase price of the target company with the applicable purchase price adjustment and payment terms are usually detailed during the negotiation of the definitive agreement for the transaction, like the merger agreement. The discussion of the purchase price begins at the LOI stage, as we discussed in the last chapter, and it continues until that negotiation and finalization of the many aspects that affect the purchase price in the merger agreement.

This chapter is all about the purchase price. I begin by discussing how a private company may be valued and how, based on that valuation, the top-line purchase price of that company is negotiated and agreed to by the parties in an M&A. Thereafter, I present examples of commonly applied adjustments to the top-line purchase price and how they result in a different take-home purchase price at the closing of the transaction. Finally, I discuss withholdings like escrows and deferred purchase price like earn-outs. The aim in this chapter is to demonstrate that there are many levers that parties can pull to create what they believe is a fair purchase price package in an M&A deal.

As a result, the top-line purchase price agreed to in the LOI can look quite different from the purchase price seller takes home at the closing of the M&A.

At the end of this chapter, I discuss how this top-line purchase price and the take-home purchase price "flows through" the capitalization table of your target company to distribute the proceeds from the sale of the company to all of the company's equity holders. A model of this flow of the purchase price down a cap table is colloquially called a "merger waterfall."

COMPANY VALUATION

After the buyer's financial due diligence (especially QofE diligence that we discussed in Chapter 3), the parties will discuss and agree on a total purchase price of the company. This is an entirely negotiated amount.

One of the questions I get most often from start-up founders is, "How do I determine the purchase price of the private company?" There are several methods for this that M&A practitioners utilize to guide their determination.

In the following, I discuss the popular methods used to arrive at the top-line purchase price and the choice of which method to use depends on the nature and industry of the target business. However, just like buying a house or a car, the price is negotiated between the parties involved and subject to current market conditions.

There are numerous methods that M&A practitioners use to ballpark the top-line purchase price of a private target company. I discuss four of the most popular methods taught in business schools. In most deals, depending on the nature of the business and the industry, parties will use a combination of these methods to inform their negotiations.

1. **Asset-Based Valuation**: This is considered the most basic valuation method, which is based on a company's net asset value (NAV). All the company's tangible and intangible assets are added up, and then all of the company's liabilities are subtracted from that total.

2. **Cost-Based Valuation**: This is also referred to as the replacement value approach or the reproduction value approach. In this method, you tally the cost of replicating the target business and use that as a basis to value the same business.

3. **Market-Based Valuation**: This is also known as the comparable company analysis. This is where you compare the target business to similar businesses in the market. If businesses similar to yours are also private companies, this market information could be hard to come by. Also, this approach does not work if you do not have reasonably comparable businesses – say by virtue of being a market disrupter.

4. **Discounted Cash Flow (DCF) Valuation**: This is also known as the income-based approach. In the DCF method, the company's value is determined by discounting the expected cash flows for the next five years to the present value of the company. If your company is prerevenue, the DCF valuation won't be applicable.

When using these valuation methods to determine the company valuation, buyers will look at some of the following key financial metrics of the company.

When you are in discussions with potential investment bankers and thereafter potential buyers, they will all ask you to share with them the following financial information about your company. It would be very helpful to have these prepared for the eventual sale of your company as part of your self-diligence.

EBITDA

EBITDA, which stands for earnings before interest, taxes,

depreciation, and amortization, is a crucial financial metric used to evaluate a company's operating performance.

$$EBITDA = Net\ Income + Interest + Taxes + Depreciation + Amortization$$

For example, if Start-Up Inc. has a net income of $2 million, interest expenses of $500,000, taxes of $300,000, depreciation of $200,000, and amortization of $100,000, the EBITDA would be $3.1 million.

EBITDA serves as a loose proxy for cash flow from the entire company's operations. It excludes the effects of financing and accounting decisions, providing a clearer picture of profitability. It also allows comparison across companies, which is why the market-based valuation method relies on EBITDA. Often, the top-line purchase price of the company is an amount that is 1x to 5x the Company's EBITDA – depending on your industry, how well your business is performing in comparison to comparable start-ups, and how attractive it is to the potential buyer.

However, EBITDA is not recognized under generally accepted accounting principles (GAAP) or international financial reporting standards (IFRS). This means it can be subject to manipulation and may not always provide a complete picture of a company's financial health. Critics of EBITDA, including Warren Buffett, argue that EBITDA ignores the cost of maintaining and sustaining capital assets, which can be significant for companies with substantial depreciable assets. As a founder, by understanding EBITDA and its applications, you can better navigate the M&A process and negotiate a fair purchase price for the company.

Net Assets

Net assets represent the total value of a company after subtracting its liabilities from its assets. This metric is crucial for the asset-based valuation method, which focuses on the company's net asset value (NAV).

Net Assets = Total Assets – Total Liabilities

For example, if a company has $10.5 million in assets and $5 million in liabilities, the NAV would be $5.5 million.

This method is particularly useful for companies with significant tangible assets, such as real estate or manufacturing firms. It provides a clear picture of what the company owns outright. In scenarios where a company is being liquidated, the NAV provides a baseline for the minimum value of the company. Private companies often use net asset valuation as part of their due diligence process to ensure all assets and liabilities are accounted for accurately.

Price-to-Earnings (P/E) Ratio

The price-to-earnings (P/E) ratio is a widely used metric that compares a company's current share price to its earnings per share (EPS). It is instrumental in the earnings-based valuation method (not listed in the common four methods above). Here's how it works:

P/E Ratio = Market Value per Share / Earnings per Share (EPS).

There are two types of P/E ratios:

1. Trailing P/E, based on past earnings
2. Forward P/E, based on projected future earnings

The P/E ratio helps investors understand the market's expectations of a company's future earnings growth. A high P/E ratio may indicate that investors expect high growth rates. The P/E ratio helps determine if a company is overvalued or undervalued relative to its peers.

Revenue

Revenue is the total amount of money received from the sales of goods or services from your target company's business activities. It is a key metric in the "times-revenue" valuation method (also not listed in the common four methods provided), which is particularly useful for young companies with volatile or nonexistent earnings.

Revenue = Price of Goods or Services x Quantity Sold

Revenue provides insight into a company's market position and growth potential. It is a straightforward metric that reflects the company's ability to generate sales. This method might value a software company at two times its annual revenue, while it might value a manufacturing factory at one time its revenue. Revenue-based valuation is ideal for companies in high-growth industries where earnings may not yet be stable.

In summary, the purchase price of your start-up will be based on your company's valuation. Your company's valuation can be surmised using various different valuation methods, each of which rely on one or more financial metrics like EBITDA or net assets.

So, in order to arrive at a fair value of your target company, you should have accurate and complete financial statements. If feasible, you should aim to make the financial statements GAAP or IFRS compliant.

PURCHASE PRICE ADJUSTMENTS

Purchase price adjustments are included in merger agreements to preserve the benefit of the parties' bargain on the purchase price during the Interim Period between signing and closing, and post-closing as well.

Here, M&A practitioners have yet to arrive at an industry-wide consensus on the specific terms used to describe each category or type of adjustment to the purchase price of a private company. As a result, you can encounter differing descriptions of the same purchase price adjustment concepts. In order to make my discussion of purchase price adjustments here less ambiguous and more useful for you, instead of attempting to describe them in words only I will work through sample calculations of the purchase price adjustment mechanisms at play. Let's continue to calculate the purchase price of Start-Up Inc., who found a buyer to purchase it for $100 million as the top-line purchase price, which was a 2x multiplier on the company valuation determined to be at $50 million.

Specified Financial Adjustments

A set of common adjustments to the top-line purchase price are specified financial items.

Most LOIs from buyers will note that the top-line purchase price they are offering is "debt free" and "cash free."

These are two types of specified financial adjustments.

Most buyers are interested only in acquiring the operating assets of the company (inventory, accounts receivable, property and equipment, etc.) and assuming its operating liabilities (accounts payable, warranties, etc.). These comprise the net operating assets that are employed to generate cash flow. However, buyers are often not interested in taking on nonoperating liabilities, such as outstanding bank loans, and they expect the seller to pay off such liabilities at or prior to the sale of the company. If Start-Up, Inc. has an outstanding loan on its books for $2 million, the $100 million purchase price would be reduced to $98 million to reflect the debt to be paid off.

Sellers, on the other hand, do not want to transfer to the buyer the cash their business has earned until the acquisition. Instead of sweeping the company's bank accounts of this cash on the eve of closing, which could lead to an operational crisis for the business, the parties agree to add this cash to the purchase price. If Start-Up Inc. has $1 million of cash in its accounts, the $100 million purchase price would be increased to $101 million to reflect the cash that is properly the seller's earnings, therefore making the buyer's acquisition cash free. There are other such financial adjustments that can be negotiated and made to the purchase price, such as the total amount of expenses incurred by the seller in hiring advisors and vendors to execute the M&A (referred to as transaction expenses). After applying these financial adjustments to the purchase price, the company arrives at a different top-line purchase price that is a more accurate reflection of the target company's value. In our example, the $100 million purchase price for Start-Up, Inc. that is debt free and cash free becomes $99 million ($2 million was subtracted as debt and $1 million was added as cash).

Adjustments to Reflect the Actual Value

A common type of adjustment that parties often negotiate adjusts the purchase price after the signing of the definitive agreement or even after the closing of the transaction. The parties use the target company's most recent financial statements to agree on a purchase price at the LOI stage, and this financial information may be an estimate at that time. In the Interim Period between signing and closing, or in a specified period after the closing of the transaction, updated financial information about the target company may become available, or changes to the target company's business or financial condition may occur, that could affect the parties' initial valuation at the LOI stage. Such purchase price adjustment allows the parties to ensure that the ultimate price paid for the target at the closing best reflects its actual value.

A recent market trend for technology M&A deals is for the parties to provide for a "two-step" adjustment to the purchase price, where an initial adjustment is calculated at the closing of the transaction based on estimated financial statements prepared by the seller then available. The second verification is another adjustment calculated at some specified time after closing by the buyer, usually within 120 days, based on the final value of the financial metric that serves as a basis for adjustment.

The net working capital (NWC) of the target company (a financial metric very closely related to NAV that I previously described) as reflected in its balance sheet is the most common basis for determining whether the purchase price has changed from the LOI to the closing of the transaction. Also,

instead of attempting to determine the actual NWC of a company at any point in time, especially for companies with variable financial performance, parties may negotiate and agree to a "target" net working capital, against which the adjustment is made.

This is commonly referred to as the working capital adjustment in an M&A.

Depending on the nature of the target's business, a different financial metric (such as NAV or net debt) or even a nonfinancial metric (such as a development milestone or other event) may be used instead of NWC. The adjustment can be based on more than one metric as well. The metrics used to serve as the basis of a post-closing purchase price adjustment will depend on the structure of the transaction and the nature of the target business being acquired.

The purchase price adjustment is typically on a dollar-for-dollar basis; for every dollar difference between the estimated base value or target value of the target business and its final value, the purchase price is adjusted upward or downward in that amount.

When the adjustment is only upward (favoring the seller) or downward (favoring the buyer),

it's called a "one-way" adjustment, and when it allows for both, it's a "two-way" adjustment.

The parties can also agree to limit the amount of the adjustment either up (setting a "cap") or down (setting a "floor") or agree that an adjustment will occur only if the difference between estimated base or target value and final value is within an agreed range of variance. Limits may be placed on the adjustments such as a minimum amount, either up or down. Now, let's put this to use in negotiating the purchase price for Start-Up Inc.

The adjusted top-line purchase price of Start-Up Inc. on a debt free, cash free basis is $99 million. The nature of Start-Up Inc.'s business is such that its NWC has been pretty stable over the last few years. So, the parties decided to have **a two-step, two-way purchase price adjustment with no limits based on a target net working capital** of $50 million. In addition, to avoid double-counting, parties agreed that any working capital calculation should exclude the repaid debt and cash already accounted for in the $99 million. At the closing, based on the latest estimated balance sheet of the closing date, Start-Up Inc.'s net working capital is estimated to be $40 million. This is $10 million less than the $50 million target, so the purchase price at the closing is adjusted downward to be $89 million. The deal closes and this adjusted purchase price (subject to any other terms) is paid to the sellers according to the agreed terms.

After closing, the buyer takes over the business and takes time to prepare the final balance sheet of Start-Up Inc. as of the closing date. Based on this balance sheet, the final net working capital of Start-Up Inc. shows that the net working capital as of the closing date was actually even lower, at $35 million! In that case, the final purchase price of the target company is $84 million. The seller now has to return $5 million to the buyer or go through the dispute resolution process that parties sometimes lay out in the event they want to contest the final purchase price determination. At the LOI stage, Start-Up Inc. started with a $100 million top-line purchase price, but after applying the agreed adjustments, the sellers get to take home only $84 million.

Let's explore some alternatives of this same fact pattern. If the parties had agreed to a single-step adjustment at the closing, then the final purchase price would have been $89 million, and there would have been no further adjustment after that. If the parties had agreed to have only an upward adjustment for the seller's benefit with no downward protection for the buyer, then the purchase price would have remained $99 million. If the parties had agreed to have a collar such that there would be no adjustment, upward or downward, beyond $3 million around the target net working capital, then the final purchase price would have been $96 million.

In the 2023 ABA M&A Deal Points Study, 92 percent of the deals analyzed had some purchase price adjustment mechanism (up from 68 percent in 2006), and of those, 89 percent were adjustments based on the net working capital of the target company, while 87 percent of the post-closing purchase price adjustments were based on more than one metric. Of such deals that relied on net working capital as a basis for post-closing purchase price adjustments, 60 percent explicitly required the closing balance sheet of the target to be in compliance with GAAP (in some form: 14 percent were compliant with GAAP but consistent with past practices, while 18 percent were compliant with GAAP with specific modifications).

I hope the foregoing discussion and illustration of

purchase price adjustments has demonstrated to you that the parties in an M&A have many types of adjustments that they can agree to for the purchase price that results in the sellers taking home an amount that is significantly different than the top-line purchase price the buyer initially offered. It is very important that you fully understand the purchase price provisions being negotiated in the M&A and ensure that you have considered the worst-case scenarios and their likelihood, in addition to the best-case ones. It is critical that your financial statements and records be in good condition for you to navigate and win the negotiation of these purchase price provisions.

ESCROW

In an M&A deal, the buyer may demand that part of the purchase price be withheld from the seller and placed in escrow or just held back by the buyer (a holdback) at closing to insure against collection risk and to ensure that funds are available to cover a seller's potential obligations to the buyer, like in the event of a downward adjustment to the purchase price. Another common and important seller obligation that an escrow or holdback can serve as partial security for is the seller's indemnification of the buyer, which we discuss in the next chapter. Parties can negotiate multiple escrows or holdbacks in a deal and set each of their terms separately. The amount of the purchase price held back and placed in escrow or holdback is likely to be a subject of significant negotiation, especially where collection risk is high. Typically, 5 to 30 percent of the top-line purchase price is placed in an escrow. The parties also negotiate the escrow period, which often tracks the survival period of the general representations and warranties provided by the seller and target company. (More on survival periods in Chapter 9.) Typically, the escrow period is twelve months to forty-eight months.

According to the 2023 ABA M&A Deal Points Study, 53 percent of the deals analyzed had a separate escrow to cover downward purchase price adjustments. Of these deals, 40 percent of the agreements provided that the escrow would be the sole source of recovery in the event of a downward purchase price adjustment by the buyer. In 19 percent of the deals where there was any escrow for purchase price adjustments, 19 percent of them had a threshold that had to be exceeded before the buyer could make a claim.

Is it bugging you that the sellers of Start-Up Inc. will now have to return $5 million to the buyer post-closing? What if they already spent the money by putting down the deposit to buy a vacation home? It's harder to let go of what we have than not to have received it in the first place. This is one of the reasons why parties to an M&A agree to an escrow or hold-back amount. In the fact pattern at the start of this chapter, we noted that Start-Up Inc. had negotiated with the buyer that 20 percent of the purchase price would be withheld at the closing of the transaction and placed in a third-party escrow account for three years to serve as security for the buyer. The parties could have also provided that this escrow would cover any downward adjustment to the purchase price following the two-step, two-way working capital adjustment.

Below is another chart illustrating the sample post-closing working capital adjustment calculations that we have been toying with for Start-Up Inc. so far and the application of an escrow to cover the purchase price adjustment.

Top-Line Purchase Price	$100 million
Debt (-)	$1 million
Cash (+)	$2 million
Estimated Top-Line Purchase Price	$99 million
Purchase Price Escrow Amount	$20 million
Estimated Top-Line Purchase Price Paid at Closing	$79 million
Target Net Working Capital	$50 million
Final Net Working Capital (post-closing)	$35 million
Remainder Paid at End of Escrow Period	$5 million
Final Take-Home Purchase Price	$84 million

DEFERRED PAYMENTS & EARN OUTS

Deferred payments are usually structured as installments to be paid after closing, either at set intervals or upon the occurrence of certain events. Some deferred payments become payable upon the meeting of certain post-closing performance milestones that are often referred to as "earn outs."

Purchase price adjustments may be distinguished from earn outs, where the buyer agrees to pay additional consideration after the transaction is closed, based on whether the acquired business achieves defined performance milestones. Earn outs are often used in situations where the parties have failed to agree on the value of the target business or when the acquired business is anticipated to grow significantly or otherwise improve after closing. Typically, earn out arrangements are seen in deals where the managers of the target business are expected to continue their involvement in the business after the closing.

Earn out arrangements have advantages and disadvantages. A clear advantage is that an earn out can help parties reach a final agreement on the purchase price even though they may disagree on the value of the target business. An earn out also allows the buyer to pay a portion of the purchase price out of the acquired business's profits after acquiring it. A disadvantage of an earn out, however, is that it can cause the parties to work at cross-purposes with respect to the post-closing operation of the acquired business. The seller may want the business to be operated in a manner that maximizes its payout under the earn out arrangement, which may or may not coincide with the buyer's long-term plans for the business. Accordingly, earn outs can be complex and time-consuming to negotiate and, ultimately, may place some restrictions on how the buyer can run the acquired business for some period of time after the transaction closes, or may include a requirement for the buyer to use certain efforts to achieve the earn out triggers.

Of the 108 deals analyzed in the 2023 ABA M&A Deal Points Study, 74 percent did not include any earn out provision, while only 26 percent of them did. Of the ones that did, revenue was the most common metric for measuring earnouts, with 58 percent of the deals relying on it. However, in only 17 percent of the these deals with earn-out provisions did the buyer agree to a covenant to run the business consistent with past practice or run the business as a stand-alone entity or division to prevent buyer's interference with the seller's ability to earn the earn out. (More on covenants in Chapters 10 and 11.)

An industry where earn outs are often used in M&A is

the biopharmaceutical research industry. Say, for example, your company is developing a very promising cancer cure drug and is only at the first clinical trial phase; you may be considering getting acquired by a Big Pharma company that can fund your research. However, the valuation of your company now will not reflect the very high valuation that you know you will be able to achieve with the funding that the buyer will give you. Similarly, on the buyer's side, they won't want to pay you the big bucks based on a potential high valuation in the future in case your trials fail regulatory approvals. In such a situation, one or more milestone payments as deferred consideration make sense where the buyer pays an amount to the seller upon achievement of certain milestones, which are negotiated.

The case of *Fortis Advisors LLC v. Shire US Holdings, Inc.* serves as an illustrative example of the complexities involved in M&A transactions, particularly concerning post-closing earn outs. Fortis Advisors LLC, acting as the stockholders' agent for the former stockholders of SARcode Bioscience Inc., alleged that Shire US Holdings, Inc. breached the merger agreement by refusing to pay certain milestone payments that were due upon the successful completion of specific development and regulatory milestones for a drug called Lifitegrast. The merger agreement between SARcode and Shire was structured to balance the risks and rewards associated with the development of Lifitegrast. The agreement included both fixed payments at closing and contingent payments or earn outs that depended on Shire's success in advancing the drug through clinical trials and obtaining regulatory approval.

This structure allowed SARcode to secure immediate financial returns while also retaining the potential for additional rewards if the drug achieved certain milestones. A key point of contention arose when Fortis believed that the milestone for the "OPUS-2" completion had been met and inquired about the corresponding $175 million deferred payment contingent on it. Shire, however, responded that the milestone had not been achieved because the OPUS-2 study failed to meet the required endpoints. Despite this, Shire continued to develop Lifitegrast and eventually obtained FDA approval for the drug under the brand name Xiidra. Following this approval, Fortis claimed that the former SARcode stockholders were entitled to both the OPUS-2 completion milestone payment and the base case approval milestone payment. However, Fortis's claims for SARcode stockholders were dismissed.

This case underscores the importance of clearly defined terms and conditions in definitive agreements, particularly regarding contingent payments and the criteria for their achievement. There is the need for careful negotiation and drafting to ensure that all parties have a clear understanding of their rights and obligations, particularly concerning contingent payments tied to future performance milestones.

Now let's take a moment to appreciate how far we have come in our journey of understanding the purchase price provisions being negotiated for the sale of Start-Up, Inc. We determined its purchase price based on the company's valuation (maybe the market-based approach based on EBITDA). Then, we negotiated specific financial terms that will adjust the purchase price and determined the correct closing and post-closing adjustment levers and any deferred payments that parties agree will lead to a fair value. We also considered escrows (and holdbacks) to serve as partial security for the buyer's collection risk against the seller's obligations. Finally, we imagined what other types of deferred payments, like earn outs, could apply if Start-Up were a biopharmaceutical research start-up. I say you are well on your way to navigating and winning purchase price discussions in an M&A.

But wait. How does one actually make these decisions in real life? How would you as the start-up founder and seller be able to decide which of these many and various purchase price terms are suitable for you, your stockholders, and your target company? Well, one of the most useful tools you can, and will, use is the merger waterfall.

MERGER WATERFALL

When you arrive at negotiating an M&A, the most important object is not a legal document but the merger waterfall. The merger waterfall is a mathematical model that shows how the purchase price is distributed to all the stakeholders of your target company in your complete and detailed cap table. Recall in Chapter 4, we discussed the capitalization of the target company and how the financing terms you agree to with your investors today, such as the liquidation preference, can affect the outcomes for you and your company's stockholders during an M&A. As you negotiate the purchase price terms with a potential buyer, you will have to understand how the competing purchase price alternatives being negotiated affect the stakeholders of your target company based on the stakeholders' existing legal and contractual rights.

Building a merger waterfall, which shows how the top-line purchase price is adjusted and then how it "flows" down the cap table of the target company to its individual or entity stakeholders is a crucial tool in modeling and understanding these competing alternatives, and helping you decide how to move forward throughout the M&A process.

As the seller, the buyer will require you to represent and warrant that the cap table of your company as of the closing date is complete and accurate. This certified cap table is the basis for the merger waterfall. Honestly, the definitive agreement will contain a lot of "legalese" that your legal advisors will negotiate and draft, based on legal precedent and driven by need. Often, this language is verbose, difficult to digest, and difficult to implement post-closing by folks who were not closely involved in the negotiation of the deal or aren't familiar with such agreements. A large part of the language comes from case law and precedent that govern the drafting, interpretation, and implementation of different types of provisions that go into the definitive agreement. Additionally, the purchase price provisions we explored earlier in this chapter are by their nature complex and multifaceted, so they often take many words to be described completely in writing. In short, even if you and your legal advisers try really hard to keep the definitive agreement "plain English," it's likely not going to be casual reading material. As a result, having the merger waterfall updated to track the evolving deal terms will help you significantly in decision-making.

Even if you rely on your legal advisor to negotiate the deal terms and explain them to you, you should personally invest time and effort in understanding how your merger waterfall works. In an M&A, the seller or target company is responsible for building the merger waterfall and delivering it at closing. Just as you certify the underlying cap table, you will also have to certify to the accuracy and completeness of your cap table calculations. You will be held liable post-closing if your cap table or any portion of the merger waterfall calculations are found to be incorrect. You, along with your investment banker and M&A lawyer, are responsible for building, updating, and finalizing the merger waterfall as you negotiate the transaction. This process of building the merger waterfall can be a major undertaking depending on the length and complexity of the deal and the target's cap table.

Despite merger waterfalls being such a critical aspect of the M&A deal, the practice currently in the industry leaves much to be desired. Merger waterfalls are often built on Excel spreadsheets (because the cap table is typically stored in Excel spreadsheet format), and their presentation, or the formulas underlying the calculations, are not standardized. The entire waterfall has to be built from scratch for each proposed transaction. Once you begin to layer in the many variations of, and limitations to, the purchase price terms, and the rights and obligations of the different equity holders in your target company, the merger waterfall can quickly become circular, complex, deeply stacked, and time consuming to edit and review.

If you hire an investment banker, they will be responsible for building the merger waterfall. However, the investment banker is not responsible for negotiating the legal terms of the deal, and as a result, they have to rely very heavily on the legal advisor to guide and review the merger waterfall. Also, each responsible party – the CEO and CFO of the target company, the corporate development team of the buyer, the legal counsel on each side, the bankers on each side, and any payment vendors – has to review each updated version of the merger waterfall and sign off on whether they accept the changes before terms can be finalized. Neither the "hot potato" method of passing around the waterfall draft from one reviewer to another, nor the "throw the wedding bouquet" method of sending a blast to everyone with each updated version from one central owner and consolidator of the waterfall, allows for seamless and efficient collaboration.

If you do not hire an investment banker, then your M&A lawyer will likely be responsible for building the merger waterfall. In my time at big law firms, building a merger waterfall was a major headache. Most associates at big law firms study law because they never want to do math. It takes even eager associates a long time to learn how to use Excel well enough to build such spreadsheets without training, because often law students don't get this technical training in law school. Clients are charged big law firm rates for the associates' time in learning or inefficiently building the merger waterfall. I myself learned to build merger waterfalls on the job. Some big law firms have attempted to solve this problem by employing accountants. Their entire job is to build merger waterfalls in house. However, they often face the same obstacle as investment bankers. They have to continue to rely on lawyers to guide them and check their work.

There is a lot of room to make the merger waterfall process in an M&A transaction more efficient, less prone to human error, and more standardized. One legal tech and fintech startup that is taking on this challenge is Merger Waterfall Inc. In the spirit of full transparency, I am a cofounder. I envisioned what I think is an ideal software technology solution to build, model, compare, share, store, and secure merger waterfalls. I hope to begin using it in my practice soon!

Ultimately, regardless of how you build the merger water-fall, starting one early in the M&A deal is immensely helpful in tracking the complexities of the purchase price provisions. A waterfall illustrates how you begin with the top-line purchase price, apply the ratio for any mixed consideration, show how specific financial items and any purchase price adjustments at the closing and post-closing will adjust the purchase price, demonstrate the effect of any withholdings in escrow and then flow the applicable amount of the purchase price to each type of equity holder on the target company's cap table down to the last dollar. I hope you appreciate how much more detailed and complex purchase price provisions can be. I have attempted to give you a general overview, but there is a lot more to this subject.

8

RISK-SHIFTING BETWEEN THE PARTIES

R isk is inherent to the endeavor of business.

Deal risk in M&A, in particular, is the possibility that certain challenges and uncertainties can arise after the closing that impacts the success of the M&A or the target company's valuation.

Here is an example of a possible negotiation of a particular deal risk – an existing set of facts about Start-Up Inc. that could result in a costly litigation matter after closing: the potential buyer in the M&A identifies during employment due diligence that the seller has a disgruntled senior employee who thinks he is being squeezed out. He is key to Start-Up, Inc.'s business, so the buyer needs to continue employing him post-closing, likely with a sweet executive compensation deal. However, the buyer believes they should not have to bear the risk of defense if the employee sues Start-Up Inc. after the buyer acquires it. The buyer wants a specific indemnity on that potential litigation matter, if it arises, and an additional 5 percent of the top-line purchase price withheld in a dedicated escrow for one year post-closing to cover this risk.

Respectfully, Start-Up Inc. does not believe there is any risk here. The employee knows he is key to the business and that a sweet hiring package is coming down the pipe for him in a potential M&A. He is not disgruntled. He is excited, as are all of the other employees at Start-Up Inc., to join forces with the potential buyer. Start-Up Inc. won't agree to this second escrow. Who is right – the buyer or seller? This is a classic example of a deal risk, where there is a possibility, but no certainty, of future loss to the buyer if buyer acquires the target company.

For me, this example demonstrates how

deal risk in an M&A is inherent to the endeavor of M&A, just like risk is inherent to the endeavor of business. Yet, buyers choose to negotiate contractual provisions that shift risk to the seller whenever possible. These are the "risk-shifting" provisions. Just like it's a win to get the maximum fair value for your target company, it's a win to take the minimum amount of risk you can negotiate in the M&A.

The sellers of Start-Up Inc. do not want to take the risk of losing an additional 5 percent of the purchase price or carry the opportunity cost of having it get locked up for one year. So, as the sellers, their goal is to address such deal risk in a different way. Ideally, the potential buyer and their counsel are appeased with the explanation Start-Up Inc. provided:

that indeed the employee is happy, not disgruntled. If not, instead of an escrow, Start-Up Inc. could offer to sweeten that employee's pot with an additional bonus from the seller's consideration (an amount much lower than 5 percent of the purchase price) in return for a partial waiver of claims by the employee against Start-Up Inc. and any of its successors. There are other solutions as well that Start-Up Inc. and its M&A lawyer can explore.

An indemnification provision, also known as a "hold harmless" provision, is used to shift potential liability resulting from deal risk from one party to the other.

You may have encountered indemnification clauses in your day-to-day commercial contracts, but it is a much simpler mechanism than what is put in place for M&As. For example, in AI licensing agreements, indemnification is crucial. Many companies are integrating AI developed in house or licensed from third parties. Even when a company develops its own AI, it will often license certain AI components from others, such as APIs for integration. Indemnification provisions in AI licenses typically cover breaches of the agreement by the counterparty. Many such AI agreements restrict how the licensed AI can be used—limiting its application to specific industries, regions, or operational scales. If the counterparty violates these terms, such as using the AI outside of agreed parameters, it constitutes a breach. With an indemnification provision, the nonbreaching party can claim damages for losses caused by the breach. These damages may include disruptions to business operations or delays in product development resulting from the unauthorized use of the AI.

Indemnification, when applied to an M&A, has certain

considerations tailored for M&A. In this chapter, I discuss some of the general legal concepts surrounding the main category of risk-shifting provisions in private company M&A – indemnification. To me, indemnification is an endlessly fascinating topic and allows for creative legal problem-solving and top-notch negotiating by your M&A lawyer. Indemnification is often considered the most complex aspect of M&A law by founders. My primary goal in this chapter is to demystify some of the key aspects of indemnification as risk-shifting provisions and help you understand why they are important. Such terms are not hypothetical discussions or dense legalese best left to lawyers; they are instead mechanisms that allow a buyer to eat into more and more of your purchase price in the event certain losses are incurred by the buyer post-closing for specified deal risk – like an employee litigation or breach of contract. This chapter will empower you to understand such risk-shifting provisions so that you can engage meaningfully in their negotiation.

INDEMNIFICATION IN M&A

Indemnification refers to the process by which parties to an M&A or third parties can bring claims based on breach of contract (the definitive agreement) after the closing of the M&A.

> **An indemnification provision in an agreement is, at its most basic, a contractual promise to cover certain losses of a counterparty that arise after closing.**

In our example for Start-Up Inc., the buyer is seeking to negotiate a special indemnification provision in the definitive agreement that lays out how the seller will cover the buyer's losses in the event the senior employee brings a litigation claim against the company post-closing. The indemnification provision the buyer proposed includes a dedicated escrow of 5 percent of the purchase price held for one year after closing.

This example demonstrates one broad category of indemnification claims: those between the parties in an M&A. The second broad category of indemnification claims are claims brought by third parties against the target company.

These claims can also be brought forward by the successor of the target company in an M&A and the basis of that claim is either a breach of the definitive agreement or the subject of a special indemnity – like the potential litigation by the disgruntled senior employee of Start-Up Inc.

Indemnification clauses are common in private company acquisitions but rarely seen in public company acquisitions. This is because a public target company typically has a large number of stockholders, and it's difficult for the buyer to locate them post-closing, making it impractical to recover losses from these public company stockholders. It is possible to not have indemnification agreements in private company acquisitions as well, where the buyer just takes on deal risk by buying the target company "as is." However, because the target private company does not have disclosure obligations as extensive as those of a public company, it's difficult for the buyer to confidently scope out any and all of the deal risk (or so they say). So, nearly all buyers will require some form of indemnity from the private target company and its sellers.

The indemnity will vary depending on the type of transaction the parties are pursuing. Most indemnification claims in M&A are brought by the buyer against the seller because the buyer is the party most likely to incur losses after taking over control of the target business after the closing of the M&A. Therefore, a buyer prefers to have broad indemnification rights. In contrast, the seller will generally want to limit indemnification as an indemnifying party. In some circumstances, however, the seller may also seek broad indemnification rights for itself, especially if the buyer is issuing stock or promissory notes as a form of consideration. In a merger of equals–type M&A transaction, where both parties in the deal are of equal size and leverage, it is possible that both parties indemnify each other similarly.

It is not possible for me to present all the details and nuance of indemnification that can be negotiated during the sale of a private company. However, I will aim to provide an overview of the key aspects of indemnification provisions that are heavily negotiated.

First, the parties will have to specify precisely which matters may form the basis of an indemnification claim and what type of losses the indemnified party will have to recover.

A common item that forms the basis of an indemnification claim by a buyer is the breach of representations and warranties by the seller. I provide an overview of representations and warranties in an M&A and how you can navigate them in the next chapter.

Second, the parties will have to set limitations on the types of recovery allowed from such claims.

For example, in the case of Start-Up Inc., if you agree to the dedicated escrow of 5 percent of the purchase price as the seller, then you want to ensure that the amount of losses you have to cover in the event the employee brings a litigation claim does not exceed the escrow amount (5 percent). This is a type of limitation on the indemnity of the buyer. I will provide an overview in this chapter of the commonly negotiated bases for indemnification claims and the limitations sellers often seek, such as a basket, deductible or cap.

To top off the discussion on limitations, I will discuss how claims of fraud can go beyond contractual limitations on indemnity.

Third, the parties will have to lay out the processes through which indemnification claims, if made, are dealt with post-closing.

I will not discuss such processes here to avoid boring you to sleep, but I will introduce you to the cottage industry in M&A of stockholder representatives who can handle such claims on your company's behalf post-closing. Let's pause and appreciate the mammoth undertaking I am contemplating here. Despite this great effort, I will only have scratched the surface of indemnification, the main type of risk-shifting provisions in an M&A. There is much more to be considered in an M&A transaction than what I discuss in this chapter or this entire book.

BASES FOR INDEMNIFICATION CLAIMS

Who Provides Indemnity

Before parties can agree on the items that are indemnified, they must first identify the party providing the indemnification (the indemnifying party). In a merger or private stock sale, the indemnifying party typically would be the stockholders of the target company prior to the transaction since the buyer owns the target company itself post-closing. In asset sales, the target company or selling entity remains a separate legal entity after closing and is available to be the indemnifying party. Nonetheless, the buyer may also require the seller's stockholders to become party to the indemnification obligations to ensure that it can collect on any losses, particularly where the seller may be liquidated after the consummation of the asset sale.

When more than one stockholder is obligated to indemnify the buyer, the parties negotiate how the liability of indemnification will be allocated among the stockholders themselves.

The buyer prefers liability for stockholders on a "joint and several" basis so that the buyer can recover all of its indemnifiable losses from any one of the stockholders instead of going to all of them, thereby reducing the buyer's administrative burden of collection. However, this is often unfair to stockholders. Instead, stockholders prefer to carry the liability of indemnity on a several, and not joint, basis, such that each stockholder is responsible according to the pro rata portion of the purchase price proceeds that they receive in the deal.

Let's continue our example. Simplify the cap table for Start-Up Inc. and assume that its ownership is as follows: Founder owns 25 percent, three investors each own 15 percent, and a large group of minority stockholders own the remaining 30 percent. In the scenario of Start-Up Inc., if the employee in question does bring a litigation claim for discrimination, then the buyer could make a claim against the key stockholders who negotiated the deal – let's say it's the founder – and expect said founder to cover all the losses of the litigation despite the fact that the founder likely received only 25 percent of the purchase price proceeds in proportion to their ownership. However, if the stockholder liability was several and not joint, then the founder would cover 25 percent of the losses from the litigation matter while the other stockholders would also cover losses according to their pro rata share of the proceeds received. Often, if the buyer insists on joint and several liability among stockholders, stockholders in an M&A can enter into a separate contribution agreement among themselves to determine how to fairly attribute the liability of indemnification.

Which Losses Are Covered

In addition to addressing the question of "Who covers the losses?," parties also have to negotiate and agree to the answer to "Which losses are covered?" This answer is the bases for indemnification claims. It is customary to cover certain types of losses by indemnity in most M&A transactions. In the following sections, I group the types of losses that are customarily covered by indemnity into three general categories.

Losses Resulting from Breaches of Representations and Warranties

Losses resulting from breaches of representations and warranties are the most common type of losses covered by indemnity. For this type of indemnity to be triggered, the indemnifying party or target company must have actually breached its representations and warranties, and losses must have resulted from that breach. I discuss representations and warranties in detail in this chapter and provide a general example here.

Landec Corporation acquired Yucatan, a guacamole company, under a Stock Purchase Agreement (SPA) for $80 million in 2018, including $15 million held in escrow for indemnification purposes. This escrow was meant to secure indemnification for breaches of representations and warranties. Yucatan made standard representations. After the acquisition, Landec discovered Yucatan had engaged in illegal activities, including wastewater dumping and bribery of Mexican officials. Landec sought indemnification from the escrow to cover remediation costs, but the equityholders, including Yucatan's founder, Ardeshir Haerizadeh, denied the claim.

Landec eventually dismissed Haerizadeh, who had been employed by the buyer post-closing as part of the acquisition. Haerizadeh then filed a wrongful termination lawsuit in 2020, while Landec countersued for fraud, breach of contract, and indemnification based on the breach of representations and warranties in the SPA. The court ruled that Landec was not required to exhaust all remedies against other parties before pursuing claims against Haerizadeh and the equity holders, and that Landec had standing to pursue its indemnification claims. According to public records this case is still being litigated.

This case highlights the critical role that representations and warranties play in M&A transactions, as they form a key basis for indemnification claims. Buyers can seek recourse for undisclosed liabilities in breach of such representations and warranties.

Losses Resulting from Breaches of Covenants

These losses are often covered by indemnity as well.

Covenants are promises to do certain acts (positive covenants) or promises to refrain from certain acts (negative covenants).

I discuss covenants in greater detail in the next two chapters. In Chapter 10, I introduce you to another subset of risk-shifting provisions – covenants – and how they can specifically relate to you continuing to provide services to the target company or its successor post-closing. In Chapter 11, I focus on a different subset of covenants, preclosing covenants or covenants that are operational during the Interim Period between signing and closing. This is another subset of risk-shifting provisions, and how they can present challenges in successfully closing an M&A deal. For now, it suffices to know that the breach of covenants made in a definitive agreement can serve as a basis for indemnification claims.

Losses Resulting from Liabilities Specific to the Transaction

Sometimes an indemnification provision will cover losses resulting from specific potential liabilities and for which the parties agreed to allocate risk between the buyer and the seller using the indemnification provisions in the definitive agreement. These matters often arise with respect to discrete issues identified during the buyer's due diligence review. The example I provided at the start of the chapter, where parties are negotiating how to cover the potential losses from a possible litigation claim by Start-Up Inc.'s senior employee, is a liability that is specific to Start-Up Inc.'s sale. Such a basis for indemnification is often referred to as a "specific indemnity." In addition to these types of transaction-specific liabilities, such an approach is not uncommon for risks associated with past tax liabilities of a target business (such that tax risks are often the subject of entirely separate indemnity provisions) and other potential liabilities for which the parties are unable to agree on the likelihood of assertion of a third party claim or the magnitude of risk exposure.

Indemnification Escrow

Let's say that for Start-Up Inc., the company won its negotiation on the specific indemnity, and it does not have a separate indemnity item or escrow in place to cover future losses for the buyer from such litigation. However, the parties had agreed that any breach of applicable law by Start-Up Inc. prior to the closing (based on the set of facts that existed before the closing of the M&A) would be the basis of an indemnification claim. This is not an uncommon basis for indemnification claims. If the employee then brings a lawsuit for discrimination against Start-Up Inc. claiming that the founder had promised him equity that was not issued prior to the M&A, the buyer could have a reasonable and alternative basis to claim coverage from seller for losses it incurs from the lawsuit. As I noted at the beginning, there can be a number of bases for indemnification negotiated between buyer and seller in the contract.

The buyer will want to ensure that the seller will be able to fulfill its indemnification obligations. One way to ensure payment is to set aside a portion of the consideration in an indemnification escrow. Recall the use of an escrow to cover the working capital adjustment to the purchase price in the previous chapter. Similarly, the same or separate escrow can be used to cover the seller's indemnification obligations and the length of such an escrow will typically track the survival period of the general representations and warranties of the seller.

LIMITATIONS TO INDEMNITY COVERAGE

The indemnity is a liability for the party that promises to cover the specified losses.

The concept of liability from breach of contract naturally exists as an unknown liability – possibly even limitless – until the parties specify its limitations in the contract.

For each basis of indemnity, parties have to specify the limitations based on the type of risk being allocated.

There exist a great many types of limitations that parties should consider putting in place for each basis of indemnification depending on the nature of the transaction and the deal risk.

This exercise of determining which limitations, and how they will be applied, will require the buyer and seller to talk to each other about any deal risk that either of them identifies. This discussion is beneficial to both parties in an M&A, especially in strategic transactions. I will discuss some commonly applied limitations to indemnification here. As the seller, you should seek to apply any and all limitations that you can to the indemnity you provide to buyer, if you provide any indemnity at all.

Survival

Apart from the items for which the indemnifying party indemnifies the indemnified party, the seller (and its stockholders, if they are indemnifying parties) will frequently attempt to limit the duration of its indemnification obligations to the buyer. This is typically accomplished by specifying in the merger agreement that all representations and warranties will expire as of a certain date and that indemnification claims related to such representations and warranties must be asserted on or before such date. Typically, the survival period for general representations and warranties ranges from six months to two years following the closing of the M&A.

The buyer's interest is in allowing itself more time post-closing to discover defects in the target business and for third-party claims to be asserted or mature to a point where losses can be ascertained. It is not uncommon to have different survival periods for different representations. For example, the agreement could provide for the applicable statute of limitations (which could be six years or more in some cases) to apply to "fundamental representations" (which we discuss in the next chapter), but a shorter survival period of one year to apply to representations whose breach can be uncovered shortly after closing, such as representations related to financial statements.

Baskets

The parties to an M&A will often attempt to limit the dollar amounts payable under an indemnification by the use of "baskets."

> **A basket requires that a party's losses exceed a threshold amount before the indemnifying party's legal obligation to cover losses is triggered.**

This allows the indemnifying party to avoid the administrative burden of responding to a claim for a small loss. Baskets come in two main varieties:

1. **Deductible**: In a deductible basket, the indemnifying party is obligated to indemnify claims only to the extent the claims exceed the threshold amount. For example, if the deductible basket is $1,000 and the claims total $1,500, the indemnifying party is responsible only for $500.

2. **First Dollar or Tipping Basket**: In a tipping basket, the indemnifying party's obligation is not triggered until the threshold amount is exceeded; but, unlike a deductible basket, the party is responsible for the entire amount of the claims once the "basket tips over." In our example above, the indemnifying party would be responsible for the entire $1,500 if the

tipping basket is $1,000, since $1,500 exceeds the
$1,000 threshold and tips the basket over.

Utilizing these two varieties of baskets, the parties can
structure an indemnity in a number of different ways. For
instance, the deductible and tipping baskets could be used
together in a "combination basket," in which there is both a
deductible and a threshold. In our example above, assuming a
$1,000 tipping basket but a $200 deductible, the indemnifying party would be responsible for $1,300. Alternatively,
the indemnification arrangement could include a "mini-
basket," which provides that claims under a certain amount
are not counted toward the triggering threshold. The mini-
basket itself could be a deductible or tipping basket. The
parties could also agree that individual claims under a certain
amount are not counted towards the calculation of a basket or
mini-basket so that negligible claims are excluded from
indemnification altogether.

Caps

The parties to an M&A will also often attempt to limit the
total dollar amount payable under an indemnification by the
use of a "cap."

> **Caps, also known as ceilings, limit a party's
> maximum total recovery to a stated dollar
> amount (typically a percentage of the purchase
> price).**

It is preferable for a seller to cap the total amount of the
losses it will cover under an indemnity to a percentage of the
purchase price. For Start-Up Inc., let's say that is 10 percent,

which means at most $10 million of the top-line purchase price would be at risk of loss under indemnity obligations in the definitive agreement post-closing.

Recall the concept of an escrow from the previous chapter. Here, Start-Up Inc. may agree to an escrow to cover its capped indemnity obligation such that $10 million (the escrow is sized according to the cap) is withheld at closing and placed in an escrow account. Such an escrow account is typically administered by a third-party vendor like an investment bank and both buyer and seller can use it to pay out any successful indemnification claims by buyer.

If there is an indemnity escrow, the buyer won't have to undertake the administrative burden of chasing stockholders of Start-Up Inc. to recover the coverage of losses owed by them under the definitive agreement. Typically, buyers will push back on any caps on indemnity and often – depending on market conditions – the overall cap on indemnity obligations of a seller could be the total amount of the purchase price proceeds that the seller actually received from the buyer in the M&A. Basically, buyers can claw back all of what they paid for the business if the total covered losses are high enough. Sellers could lose all the payments they received in the deal!

Additionally, the buyer will resist caps. They may want to make distinctions between different kinds of deal risk and which ones are subject to caps (and which not) and, if subject to a cap, then what that amount should be. The buyer will want certain kinds of losses, such as breaches of fundamental representations and warranties and breaches of covenants, excluded from any general cap on indemnity or be made subject to a higher amount.

There are many different kinds of limitations to an indemnity that parties in an M&A can fashion to strike an agreeable deal on who carries a specified risk in the deal. We are not going to be able to explore all the possible kinds of limitations here. However, there is one unique feature of these indemnification provisions that makes it particularly valuable for you to know them. Sometimes, the indemnification provisions in the contract can be only remedy that you agree to provide to a buyer. More on this in the next chapter. This is a good thing because by default under common law a buyer can ask for all kinds of remedies, like specific injunction where they can compel you to undertake an act or omission to remedy the damage caused by the breach.

Limits on a party's, typically the seller's, indemnification obligations are some of the most heavily negotiated provisions in an M&A because it goes to the heart of which party carries the deal risk in the M&A. As I demonstrated, there are many varieties of limitations that the parties should consider and agree to in order to fairly attribute risk during an M&A deal. However, alternatively, buyers can choose to just buy the company "as is" and not negotiate any of these contractual provisions that address deal risk – because risk is inherent to the conduct of business.

PROCESS OF BRINGING CLAIMS

The indemnification section of a definitive agreement typically includes a fairly detailed mechanism for the resolution of claims, including the type of notice of a claim that needs to be given, the timing by which such notice must be given, and the process for resolving claims.

The mechanism usually draws a distinction between claims relating to losses incurred by the indemnified party, and claims relating to

losses incurred by a third party (neither the buyer nor the seller) for which such third party is seeking recovery from the indemnified party.

We will not go into details of such logistics here, but I will mention the role of the stockholder representative in representing the seller post-closing when a buyer brings indemnity claims.

Stockholder Representative

A stockholder representative, also known as a shareholder or equity holder representative, is the representative of the sellers in an M&A transaction post-closing. In smaller deals with a closely held cap table, often the CEO of the target is the stockholder representative post-closing. However, for a CEO who will continue working at the target business for the buyer post-closing, this could present a conflict. The CEO will be incentivized to maintain a professional relationship with his new employer, and this could conflict with his duty to defend the best interests of the sellers or all of the stockholders of the target business. It may also be a lot of work to engage on post-closing matters that the CEO, or other stockholders, may not have the capacity to take on. In such a scenario, it may be advisable for the seller to hire a professional service company, like SRS Acquiom or Fortis Advisors, who can provide stockholder representative services for a fee. Additionally, a professional stockholder representative can bring expertise and resources that may not be readily available to individual stockholders.

Stockholder representatives, whether paid or not, play a crucial role. The stockholder representative is appointed to act on behalf of the former or selling stockholders of the target. They serve as the single point of contact for the buyer and handle post-closing matters and disputes, such as indemnification claims. By taking on the role, the stockholder representative helps mitigate personal and professional risks for individual stockholders. This is especially important if post-closing litigation arises, as the representative can handle these complexities on behalf of stockholders by ensuring that the interests of the stockholders are protected. Stockholder representatives also help to ensure that full payments are made after closing and that all contractual obligations are met.

Recall our study of the *Shire US Holdings* case in the previous chapter where Fortis Advisors was the stockholder representative litigating on behalf of the biotech company to claim earn outs under the acquisition agreement. In sum, a stockholder representative is essential in ensuring a smooth transition and protecting the interests of selling stockholders in an M&A transaction. As a start-up founder, you should consider whether you want to take on this additional work or pay to hire a professional stockholder representative.

In the *Landec-Yucatan* dispute, Haerizadeh argued that Landec's claims should only be asserted against the stockholder representative that the sellers had hired in the deal (and not the stockholders or himself), as provided by the SPA. The California court determined that while Landec had the option to pursue claims through the stockholder representative, it was not required to do so. Landec could bring claims directly against the stockholders. Typically, a claimant bringing a lawsuit under breach of indemnification provisions in a definitive agreement in a merger will name the stockholder representative and sellers or stockholders as the plaintiffs; regardless, it is the sellers or stockholders who are party to the transaction that will be found liable for paying losses (and not a stockholder representative).

FRAUD

One of my pet peeves in negotiating an M&A transaction is frustration at how often, and how much time, other M&A lawyers tend to spend negotiating the theoretical ins and outs of "fraud." To be clear, it is an extremely important concept to understand and there is deep case law on the subject since fraud is likely to appear in most post-closing claims about an M&A. M&A practitioners can, and have, written entire books on the subject of fraud in M&A transactions.

However, for our purposes, I am going to focus on the two key takeaways for a start-up founder: (1) Try your best to not commit fraud when selling your start-up, and (2) if you believe there is some basis for a buyer or third party to allege that you committed fraud, be forthcoming with your M&A lawyer. In such a scenario, your M&A lawyer may advise you to engage a business litigation expert in your applicable jurisdiction. In order to understand why I am making these recommendations, it will be helpful for you to understand, generally, what fraud is and how it can play a role in private company M&A.

Fraud exists as a common law remedy for parties.

This common law right to not be defrauded exists outside the contract and does not need to spelled out in writing between the parties. In a private company M&A, the concern is that the buyer will allege that seller committed fraud in connection with the sale of the target business. In order to make such a claim for fraud in a transaction governed by Delaware law, the buyer will have to demonstrate the following elements are true:

1. The seller made a false representation, usually one of fact;
2. The seller had knowledge or belief that the representation was false, or made it with reckless indifference to the truth;
3. The seller had an intent to induce the buyer to act or to refrain from acting;
4. The buyer took actions (or inaction) in justifiable reliance on the representation; and
5. The buyer suffered damages as a result of such reliance.

These elements of fraud can be altered to some extent by the parties to an M&A through contractual terms in the definitive agreement. A buyer often prefers to leave the concept of common law fraud as is, without further amendment in the definitive agreement. This is because the common law concept is broad and goes beyond the requirement that you need to intentionally commit fraud. The common law concept of "fraud" includes a much broader basis for liability, like recklessness where it's sufficient for a person to just be negligent, instead of intentional, when committing fraud.

However, a seller often prefers to define fraud as applicable to that M&A not just to limit its definition, but because it is then easier to understand and negotiate "carve outs" for fraud. A fraud carve out provides an exception

for fraud to limitations that apply to indemnity
(some of which I previously noted).

The two primary types of fraud carve outs in definitive agreements are public policy fraud carve outs based on state law and express fraud carve outs negotiated between the parties in the definitive agreement. A typical, express fraud carve out proposed by a buyer in a private company M&A is that a buyer's losses resulting from fraud committed by the seller is not subject to any caps or limits, and such losses may even exceed the total purchase price proceeds received by the seller in an M&A.

This means that if a seller is found to have committed fraud, then the seller may end up paying even more out of pocket than what the seller received for the sale of the company. If fraud is undefined and left to common law in such a situation, the risk to the seller can be even higher since the fraud claim can turn what would otherwise be an indemnity claim subject to negotiated baskets and caps into an uncapped tort-based fraud claim, due to the recklessness element, even if the fraud was unintentional. Let's discuss a popular case study here.

In August 2013, UBC agreed to sell three of its pharmaceutical research and development businesses to Bracket for $187 million under a securities purchase agreement (SPA).[1] The SPA included a provision that limited Bracket's remedy for breaches of representations and warranties to an insurance policy (RWI Policy), except in cases of deliberate fraud and

---

1. The case of *Express Scripts, Inc. v. Bracket Holdings Corp.* (2021) involves United BioSource LLC (UBC), a subsidiary of Express Scripts Inc. (ESI), and Bracket Holding Corp. (Bracket), a holding company formed by Parthenon Capital Partners LP for the acquisition.

certain fundamental representations. After the closing, Bracket alleged that ESI and UBC had engaged in fraud by inflating the revenue and working capital of one of the acquired divisions. Bracket claimed that the target company's financials were misrepresented, leading to an overpayment for the acquisition. Bracket initially recovered $13 million under the RWI Policy through arbitration for breach of the SPA's representations and warranties. Subsequently, Bracket sued ESI and UBC for fraud in Delaware Superior Court, where a jury awarded Bracket over $82 million. ESI and UBC appealed the jury verdict and judgment to the Delaware Supreme Court.

The Delaware Supreme Court's holding in this case was that the Delaware Superior Court had erred in its jury instruction by allowing the jury to find for Bracket based on recklessness, rather than deliberate fraud, which was a key provision of the SPA. The Supreme Court emphasized that a deliberate state of mind is distinct from recklessness and that the erroneous instruction violated the SPA's terms and the parties' risk allocation. Consequently, the court reversed the Superior Court's judgment and remanded the case for a new trial. The court's decision here gives us assurance that, if a litigation matter arises, then importance is placed on adhering to the specific terms in a definitive agreement like the SPA regarding the limitation of remedies and the distinction between deliberate fraud and recklessness in the context of M&A transactions.

However, given the fact-specific nature of a court's analysis during fraud claims in M&A, not all outcomes are so reassuring. Additionally, the Delaware courts have had many opportunities to opine on this area of the law and there are various factors to consider when negotiating fraud carve outs in M&A transactions. This is a complex and nuanced area of law. You should rely on your M&A lawyer to explain the fraud-related laws and provisions relating your M&A.

MORE WAYS TO TAKE BACK PURCHASE PRICE PROCEEDS

There are simply too many nuances under the law in negotiating indemnification provisions, or risk-shifting provisions, in an M&A. I have explained to you the importance of risk-shifting provisions in an M&A and how it can eat away at your purchase price post-closing. I have provided high-value and high-impact limitations to indemnification claims that you as a seller should aim to negotiate in an M&A deal. I have also provided a general overview of the key process issues in enforcing indemnification claims. However, this is hardly enough to ensure you are properly protected from deal risk during an M&A.

I end the chapter on risk-shifting provisions by discussing fraud because sometimes, if a seller may be found liable for fraud in selling the company, the seller's risk may be high and often such risk cannot be contracted away. This is a good segue into our next chapter on representations and warranties and their role in risk-shifting between the buyer and seller. So far, we have discussed numerous instances where the nature and scope of representations made by the seller has affected how much risk – and loss – they were subject to. The next chapter will dive into representations and warranties in detail and end with discussing the concept of representations and warranties insurance (RWI) as an alternative to contractual risk-shifting between the parties in an M&A.

9

REPRESENTATIONS AND DISCLOSURES

L et's go back to our dating analogy for a change of pace. When you are a few months into a whirlwind romance with a potential partner who seems like he is the perfect match, you start sharing private information to get to know each other better. During a dinner date, the potential partner asks you if you have ever gotten into a car accident. In fact, you had as a teenager gotten a DUI conviction for driving into your neighbor's mailbox while drunk. You know that your date was also witness to a car accident. A drunk driver ran over his childhood pet. You know your response to your date's question could break the relationship. You know you are a responsible driver now, so you decide to skip over the story of your DUI conviction.

Fast-forward years later, when you are happily married to your former date. You are asked to serve on a jury and your husband offers to generously drive you to the jury selection and keep you company. During the selection, he learns in public from a stranger trial attorney of your prior DUI conviction as a teenager as you are dismissed from the jury panel for this trial of a drunk driver who killed an elderly individual.

Now, imagine this partner is actually your strategic buyer, who learns after acquiring your start-up that you had knowingly lied about, or hid, a fact regarding the target business that you knew was important for the buyer in deciding whether to buy your company. They could walk away from the deal and bring a lawsuit against you.

As I discussed in the previous chapter, this could very well be the basis for the buyer to bring an indemnification claim against you for breach of a representation or warranty under the definitive agreement or even bring a common law tort claim for fraud. If a buyer believes they have been wronged and a seller misrepresented the target business or its value – and they have sufficient evidence to back it – the buyer would be well within their rights to pursue the seller for recovery of monetary damages.

What would such a buyer say? He would say you lied about the target business and point to the written record of where you lied.

That record of what you told the buyer about your target business, which the buyer relied on when entering into the M&A, is the representations and warranties section of the definitive agreement and its related disclosure schedules.

A critical part of the risk you carry as a seller of a start-up in an M&A for an indemnification claim is the underlying representation or warranty the buyer will claim you breached. The subject, nature, and scope of the representation and warranty dictates the risk you carry for its potential breach.

As a seller, you can use the representations and warranties about the target business, and its attendant disclosure schedules, as an avenue to air any known or perceived facts about the target company to the buyer and thereby minimize the risk of a post-closing claim.

This chapter is a complement, and addition, to the previous chapter. In this chapter, I introduce you to the concepts of representations and warranties and disclosures. Then, I will discuss the intriguing concept of "sandbagging," which ties the representations and warranties you make as a seller to the risk that you carry under indemnification provisions in a definitive agreement. To keep the text readable, I will refer to "representations and warranties" as just "reps" in this chapter. Finally, I will end the chapter with a primer on representations and warranties insurance (RWI) policies and when that can serve as an alternative to risk-shifting between the buyer and seller in an M&A.

REPRESENTATIONS AND WARRANTIES

Representations and warranties, or "reps," are statements of fact, not promises.

To be exact, reps are statements of fact that generally relate to past or present facts, while warranties generally relate to future facts and what will be true. In that way, warranties are more like promises. However, in the United States, M&A practitioners do not generally distinguish between the two. They address representations and warranties or just reps as a whole: statements of fact that relate to past, present, and future facts. The seller in an M&A usually provides substantially a lot more reps than the buyer. Often, especially if stock is a part of the deal consideration, the buyer will also provide detailed reps to the seller. In a merger of equals deal, the substantiality of the buyer's and seller's reps are similar. The nature and scope of the reps provided by each party to the transactions depends on the size, complexity, and structure of the M&A transaction and each party's leverage.

You have likely encountered reps already in the conduct of your business. If you have raised money for your start-up, you have likely provided reps about your start-up and target business to investors in a stock purchase agreement or to lenders in a loan agreement. In particular, the reps in an M&A are very comprehensive and extensive because buyers seek reps about each aspect of the target business, like intellectual property, tax, human resources, property – the list appears endless. The stockholders of the target company or sellers may have to provide additional reps about themselves, like their authority to sell the company, in addition to reps about the target business. In a deal with separate signing and closing, parties will provide the reps in the definitive agreement as of the signing date and then once again make the same reps as of the closing date at closing through a mechanism called the "bring-down" of reps. According to the 2023 ABA M&A Deal Points Study, 66 percent of the deals surveyed required the target reps to be accurate at both the signing and closing (bringing down the reps at closing), while 33 percent only required the reps to be accurate at closing only. The reps are often the longest portion of a merger agreement.

Negotiations of representations and warranties will revolve around content, scope, and the use of qualifiers. A buyer will typically want you to provide the broadest reps possible about the target business without any qualification. As a seller, your goal is to narrow the scope of reps in a manner that fits your target business – often called "ringfencing."

The initial draft of the definitive agreement from the buyer's counsel often contains a general set of extensive, standard reps about the business and it is your task to advise your M&A lawyer on how to tailor the reps to fit your business and the transaction. You should include reasonable limitations to your reps that appropriately represent the materiality, knowledge, and range of the facts about the target business you are able to stand behind. Such qualifiers are often heavily negotiated since they narrow the basis for indemnification claims by the buyer. Both of these qualifiers therefore shift the risk of immaterial or unknown breaches of the reps from the party giving the reps (often the seller) to the party receiving the reps (often the buyer). A seller in an M&A must ensure that its reps are accurate and complete without appropriate qualifications to minimize risk.

Fundamental Reps

I will spend the least amount of time possible discussing the nature and scope of the representations and warranties a private company will provide in an M&A other than to highlight fundamental reps. This is because there is no particular trick involved in gaming the nature and scope of general reps – the buyer will want the seller to rep about every possible aspect of the target business. I want to spend our time discussing the concepts that can directly affect your bottom line – or as I call it, the take-home purchase price – when and after you sell your start-up. Some of the most common reps made by sellers relate to facts about the financial health of the target business. For example, according to the 2023 ABA M&A Deal Points Study: 97 percent of the deals surveyed had a rep stating that the financial statements of the target company fairly presents the financial condition of the target business; 96 percent had a rep stating that the target has no liabilities other than those reflected in its balance sheet; and 100 percent had some form of a rep stating that the target conducts its business in compliance with all applicable laws.

Fundamental reps are a particular set of representations and warranties that relate to a party's corporate status and authority to enter into the transaction. Fundamental reps are often statements of fact about the seller's corporation organization and good standing, authority to enter into the merger agreement, and the capitalization of the target company. We discussed some key fundamental reps relating to corporate governance and capitalization in Chapter 4.

The reps are considered so fundamental to an M&A that most often, fundamental reps are not subject to any limitations to indemnification that I list in the previous chapter or any qualifiers to reps that I go on to discuss.

So, as you read the qualifiers to reps that I provide, please keep in mind that such qualifiers are often not applied to fundamental reps.

Materiality

> **A rep can be qualified by what is material or what might cause a material adverse event to the target business. "Material" generally refers to facts or information that a reasonable investor would consider important in making a decision about the transaction.**

This standard is consistent with the definition used in securities law, where materiality is judged by whether a reasonable investor would attach importance to the fact in question when making an investment decision. Materiality qualifiers are used to avoid triggering insignificant breaches of the reps. For example, the target company might rep to the buyer that the start-up is not a party to any legal action before a governmental body. Under this broad rep, the buyer may claim that the start-up is in breach of this rep when it finds out that the start-up was subject to a tax audit before the Internal Revenue Service (IRS). Any legal action before a government body, no matter how small, can be swept into this broad rep. However, if the target company reps instead that it is not a party to any *material* legal action before a governmental body, the buyer is then unable to claim post-closing that the start-up is in breach of this rep when it finds out that the start-up was subject to a tax audit before the IRS if the consequence of such an audit would be, or is, insignificant to the target company. Materiality qualifications make it easier for the start-up to focus on reps about facts or omissions that are important to the target business. It is easier for the start-up to check and verify.

Most of the founders I advise are rightly confused by what could count as "material" in a particular context. In our example, if there is an ongoing tax audit of your start-up the outcome of which you suspect would be inconsequential to the target company's finances, but you cannot be sure, is it material enough to disclose under the materiality-qualified rep that your start-up is not a party to any legal action before a governmental body? Honestly, your M&A lawyer wouldn't be able to opine on such gray areas because materiality is a decision that requires knowledge of the target business. In such situations, I encourage my clients to be biased toward disclosure to ensure the risk lies with the buyer – who cannot later claim that they didn't know. More on this in the sand-bagging section. Parties in an M&A often seek to specify a materiality standard by adding a dollar threshold to a rep. For example, instead of repping that the target company is not a party to any material legal action before a governmental body and being stressed about what could be material, the rep could state that the target company is not a party to any material legal action before a governmental body that seeks damages or costs of $10,000 or more.

The parties may also choose to employ materiality qualifiers using the defined term "Material Adverse Change" or "Material Adverse Effect" (often referred to as a "MAC" or "MAE"). This is often the highest and hardest to meet of the materiality qualifiers because the parties negotiate specific market and economic conditions that informs the MAC/MAE and the Delaware courts only once in its history of litigation about M&A has found the existence of facts sufficient to be a MAC/MAE. Most MAC/MAE definitions are formulated as any event, change, or condition that is materially adverse to the financial condition, business, or results of operations of the target business. The seller reasonably wants to limit the application of the MAC/MAE and thus will seek to negotiate carve outs from the MAC/MAE definition.

For instance, the seller may request carve outs for events that can have a material adverse effect on the target business but are industry-, market-, or transaction-related and not specific to the fundamentals of the target business, including changes affecting the target's industry generally; changes to the financial or securities markets or economic, regulatory, or political conditions, acts of God, pandemics, or wars and terrorist attacks; changes in applicable law, accounting principles, or interpretations thereof; and actions taken by the target that were required by the merger agreement or approved by the buyer. The goal for the seller is to not get penalized when they inadvertently breach a rep due to a MAC/MAE that was not of the seller's making.

According to the 2023 ABA M&A Deal Points Study, 95 percent of the deals surveyed had a defined MAE/MAC qualifier, and 93 percent of the deals surveyed had a buyer-friendly carve-out that allowed application of such MAE/MAC standard to forward-looking events that "could reasonably be expected to have" a material adverse effect on the target business.

As a founder and CEO of the target business, you will have to use your business judgment to determine whether a fact or omission about the target business is material and how to best qualify the materiality when considering such a qualification to the reps regarding such fact or omission. This will effectively shift the risk of that qualified rep from the sellers if your target business (which includes you) to the buyer.

Knowledge

A rep can also be qualified by what a party knows or should know – such that the statement of fact is true insofar as the party making

the statement knows, or should know, it to be true.

Parties often negotiate who has the knowledge and what counts as "knowledge" in such a context. Knowledge qualifiers are generally appropriate when it cannot reasonably be expected that the representing party will be aware of those certain facts related to its target business. For example, the start-up stockholder's reps relating to product and intellectual property of the target business is qualified by the knowledge of the chief technology officer (CTO) of the start-up, who knows about such facts instead of, say, the stockholders of the target business. These "knowledge persons" then must review the reps they are responsible for providing to ensure their completeness and accuracy.

Parties may also negotiate and establish the level of "knowledge" necessary for the qualifier to work. The seller should want an actual knowledge standard – that is, in order to be in breach of the rep, the seller must affirmatively know that the rep is false. However, buyers claim that proving actual knowledge of a seller is extremely difficult – just short of an admission by the seller that they knew a rep to be false. Moreover, buyers argue that a seller will be disincentivized to perform further investigations or obtain updated data on its business and financial condition prior to closing due to reliance on the knowledge qualifications.

The buyers' fears are often unsubstantiated, but they push for a more expansive knowledge standard that includes "constructive" or "imputed" knowledge in addition to actual knowledge. The buyer can want the knowledge standard to include any knowledge that the representing party would have after "due inquiry" or "reasonable inquiry." This approach raises the additional question of what constitutes due or reasonable inquiry? M&A practitioners generally agree that due inquiry means, at a minimum, officers and directors of the seller speaking with those managers or other employees who are responsible for the subject matter covered by the qualified reps.

For example, going back to our rep on litigation, the target company might rep that to the knowledge of its CEO, the start-up is not a party to any legal action before a governmental body. Then, after closing, when the buyer finds out that the target company had received a letter informing it that it is now subject to the tax audit by the IRS, the standard of knowledge would play a critical role. If the standard is actual knowledge and the CEO did not actually know about the letter, then there is no breach of the rep. If the standard is due inquiry and the CEO did not ask its tax agent about whether the tax agent could confirm the rep to be true and therefore didn't know about the letter, then there can be a breach of the rep.

According to the 2023 ABA M&A Deal Points Study, 92 percent of the deals surveyed had some form of the constructive knowledge qualifier, while 7 percent had the actual knowledge qualifier and 1 percent were undefined. Of the 92 percent of the deals that had a constructive knowledge qualifier, they used the reasonable or due inquiry standard.

Scrapes

Imagine now that you have gone through the painstakingly detailed process of reviewing the seller's reps – the statements of fact (or omissions) – about your target business and thoroughly negotiated the materiality and knowledge qualifiers to such reps to ensure that the reps are complete and accurate, and you have fairly shifted the risk of such immaterial or unknown risks to the buyer. You feel good about it. However, your M&A lawyer is getting all worked up and harping on about "materiality scrapes" that the buyer insists on adding to the indemnification provisions. Here, I explain to you why scrapes are critical to the deal risk you carry.

Where the seller's reps have materiality qualifiers, the buyer is concerned that it will suffer losses resulting from inaccuracies of those reps that are immaterial. Individually each loss from a breach of a rep may be immaterial, but in the aggregate, these losses may be significant. This phenomenon is of particular concern if there is a basket limiting the breach of indemnity for that rep; so long as the inaccuracies do not reach a material level, the losses may still not count toward the basket amount necessary to trigger the indemnification obligation.

So, buyers often seek to "scrape" off these materiality and knowledge qualifiers to the reps when determining whether the seller's indemnity obligations are triggered under the definitive agreement.

A scrape can be applied to either or both materiality and knowledge qualifiers. Such a materiality scrape can be structured to read out materiality qualifiers for purposes of determining whether a breach of a rep has occurred, or when calculating the amount of losses suffered from said breach, or for both of these exercises. When a scrape is applied to both the determination of a breach of rep and calculating its losses it's called a "double scrape" and when it's only used to determine one of these it's called a "single scrape." In the latter situation, the scrape overlaps significantly with indemnification limitations, such as baskets and caps that I detailed in the previous chapter, to present the final outcome of the indemnification obligations.

As a seller, the ideal outcome is that you have no such scrapes in the definitive agreement so that your hard work in qualifying the reps appropriately translates to shifting the deal risk to the buyer. However, market trends often inform the negotiation of such terms like scrapes. Currently, it is quite common to actually have some single or double materiality scrape included in a definitive agreement but balanced out with a basket or a mini-basket to prevent the seller from having to covering insignificant losses. A savvy M&A lawyer will keep up with these market trends and employ them to your advantage in crafting such indemnification limitations.

DISCLOSURE SCHEDULES

As we noted earlier, there is significant interplay between the negotiation of representations and warranties in an M&A and the due diligence process. As the parties provide each other with information about their respective businesses and financial condition, the draft reps will be expanded or pared back as appropriate. The parties can spur each other to disclose certain information through the drafting and negotiations of the reps to support, complement, or ensure the information obtained and disclosed in due diligence. Information gathered through the due diligence process also is used to prepare disclosure schedules.

"Disclosure schedules" are addenda to the representations and warranties in which certain factual disclosures relating to such representations and warranties are made.

In our example of the sellers of a start-up repping to the fact that the target company is not a party to any legal action before a governmental body, the seller can choose to qualify this rep by adding a disclosure. If the target company is indeed party to such an action, like a tax audit by the IRS, the sellers should rep that the target company is not a party to any legal action before a governmental body except as provided in the litigation schedule and in that schedule provide facts about the tax audit by the IRS. This disclosure then makes the litigation rep accurate and complete.

There are two main types of disclosure schedules.

The first type sets forth exceptions to a particular rep that would otherwise make the rep inaccurate.

Sometimes, the buyer will explicitly call out the information they want disclosed in the schedules to the rep thereby making them required disclosures. For example, buyers often ask for disclosure schedules that lists the following (among many others): jurisdictions in which the target company is qualified to do business; names of the company's directors and officers; contracts of the company generating revenue of $10,000 or more per year; and IDs of the company's employees and their salaries and benefits.

The second type discloses information required to complete a rep, often referred to as "voluntary disclosures."

This type of schedule is a source of information about the business or assets to be acquired that the buyer may not have otherwise discovered, or would not have been able to discover, on its own. Voluntary disclosures are a great way for you to shift the risk to a potential buyer. In our running example, let's say the sellers of the start-up made a rep that the target company is not a party to any material legal action before a governmental body. Here, the target company is subject to a tax audit by the IRS where the founder is not sure whether it is material enough to trigger a required disclosure under the rep. However, the founder can choose to inform the buyer about this deal risk anyway by making a voluntary disclosure of the facts about the tax audit in the litigation schedules supporting the rep. The buyer can, of course, push back on this voluntary disclosure if it is not willing to assume the risk. The buyer can also take the position that the facts do not require disclosure by the rep if it's immaterial or it should be subject to a specific indemnity – a concept we discussed in the previous chapter – to ensure buyer is covered for any losses from a breach of such rep post-closing.

Due Diligence and Disclosures

Founders sometimes confuse the buyer's due diligence, which we discussed in Chapter 4, with the seller's preparation of the disclosure schedules. During due diligence, the start-up provides copious amounts of information to the buyer through a "data room," on calls, by email, through advisor and counsel, or by physical review or transfer of documents. The buyer then uses the same information to review the reps provided by the seller and the attendant disclosure schedules prepared by the seller. In practice, this overlap can be a confusing experience for a seller.

In a "European-style" M&A deal, the information that a start-up provides in response to the buyer's due diligence is automatically a part of the reps in the definitive agreement and considered disclosed as if fully set out in the disclosure schedules. This simplifies the process for the seller and shifts risk to buyer efficiently. However, in the United States, the information provided during due diligence is separate from the reps. Each fact or contract has to be listed in the disclosure schedules with specificity by the seller to be considered disclosed.

In the United States, reps serve several key roles. For the buyer, they confirm the accuracy of the seller's business attributes and act as insurance for the buyer's due diligence. In private company M&A, where public information on the target is limited, the reps are the primary source of actionable information. The seller's willingness to make detailed reps can help induce the buyer to proceed with the transaction. In most US deals, the parties will disclaim responsibility for the accuracy of the information exchanged, except as reflected in the reps and disclosure schedules.

Despite the legal distinction between reps and due diligence in the United States, there is a significant interplay between the two. Due diligence findings often inform the negotiation of reps and disclosures, directing where the buyer should focus further investigation.

Preparing disclosure schedules is a painstaking and labor-intensive process due to its detailed nature. Since the reps and schedules concern facts about the target business, responsibility for preparing the disclosure schedules often falls on business owners or executives like you. Your M&A lawyer will help you understand and interpret the reps so that you and your staff can identify and disclose all relevant information. As a founder, it's important to prepare your team for the task of preparing disclosure schedules.

TYING IT TOGETHER

So far in this chapter, you have learned what reps in a definitive agreement are and how they affect the deal risk by being the basis for indemnification and fraud claims that I introduced and discussed in the previous chapter. As the founder of the start-up being sold in such an M&A, you have also learned how to mitigate the risk of being subject to indemnification or fraud claims by the buyer post-closing by crafting the scope of the reps you provide to fit the target business by applying appropriate materiality and knowledge qualifiers and negotiating any scrapes in connection with other limitations to indemnification. You also learned how to use disclosure schedules as an avenue to make required and voluntary disclosures that make the reps accurate and complete – thereby shifting risk to the buyer.

In this section, I combine the concepts of indemnity and fraud from the previous chapter with the reps and disclosures I present so far in this chapter to outline two areas where sellers should seek to confirm that their risk from breach of reps is mitigated. One area is the combination of antireliance and exclusive remedy provisions, and another area is sandbagging.

Antireliance and Exclusive Remedy

An important part of limiting the seller's reps within the definitive agreement is ensuring there is an antireliance provision provided by the seller. An antireliance provision under Delaware law is a contractual clause that explicitly states the parties do not rely on any representations or statements made outside the written agreement. Both buyer and seller can provide antireliance provisions, but these provisions typically benefit the seller, who often provides more extensive representations about the target business.

In addition to antireliance, parties can also agree to an exclusive remedy provision, where the contractual indemnification terms negotiated by the parties become the buyer's exclusive remedy for seeking coverage for losses. This is an important tool to ensure limitations on indemnification apply in an M&A transaction. If the buyer agrees to contractual indemnity as the exclusive remedy, they are generally prevented from seeking other remedies not included within the indemnity language. Indemnity, fraud, antireliance, and exclusivity all work together to form a comprehensive risk-shifting framework, and their interplay is subject to negotiation in each deal.

In a key Delaware Supreme Court case, *Fortis Advisors LLC v. Johnson & Johnson* (2022), the court emphasized that exclusive remedy provisions do not bar fraud claims based on extracontractual representations unless there is express antireliance language in the contract. This indicates that sellers should pair antireliance with exclusive remedy to minimize deal risk from breach of reps. Delaware courts maintain a strong public policy against intentional fraud, so any provision attempting to limit liability for fraud is closely scrutinized. The court made clear that while parties can draft provisions to limit liability, these provisions must be explicit. Specifically, the court noted that no Delaware court has found an exclusive remedy provision to bar a plaintiff from bringing a fraud claim based on extracontractual representations in the absence of express antireliance language. This principle recognizes that sophisticated parties can limit their reliance on representations made outside the contract, but they must do so clearly and unambiguously.

This case highlights that in an M&A transaction where

there are significant extracontractual representations a buyer might rely on, the seller's counsel should explicitly limit those representations to the four corners of the definitive agreement. This provision is crucial to reducing the risk of future fraud or misrepresentation claims based on statements made outside the agreement, as illustrated by the *Johnson & Johnson* case.

Sandbagging: Pro or Anti?

A final key legal concept that I think you should know that affects your deal risk in connection to representations and warranties is sandbagging.

In private transactions,

"sandbagging" occurs when one party (usually the buyer) learns of a breach of the other party's representations and warranties, closes on the transaction anyway, and then asserts an indemnification claim against the other party (usually the seller) for breach of such reps. Ouch.

Let's say in our running example, the sellers of the start-up made a rep that the target company is not a party to a material legal action before a governmental body. The buyer pushed back and did not want the sellers to disclose the tax audit by the IRS to the litigation schedules. However, in engaging in negotiations about whether to disclose this tax audit by the IRS, the buyer actually learned about the existence of the tax audit and was able to diligence its risk. Then, after closing the transaction, the buyer turns around and sues the sellers for breach of the litigation rep. Here, the buyer is "sandbagging" the sellers. As a seller, this does not feel good.

To protect themselves from this possibility, sellers often seek to include an "anti-sandbagging" provision, in which the buyer represents that, as of the signing or closing or both where the seller provides the reps, the buyer has no knowledge of any fact or occurrence that would lead it to conclude that a seller rep has been breached. An anti-sandbagging provision is designed to undercut any argument by the buyer that it closed the transaction in reliance on the seller's reps on paper while there is an actual or potential breach of a seller's rep existing outside the confines of the merger agreement. The seller will argue that, if the buyer knows of a breach, it should work with the seller to remedy such breach prior to closing the M&A.

The buyer, on the other hand, will object to an anti-sandbagging provision because the provision could lead to protracted disputes over what the buyer knew or should have known before closing. One way to remedy this is to apply an actual knowledge standard for the buyer's anti-sandbagging representation. See how the concepts of a definition of knowledge as actual knowledge is used to qualify a buyer's rep such that the rep shifts deal risk from seller to the buyer?

The buyer could also perceive the seller's request for an anti-sandbagging provision as a dog whistle for a costly loss post-closing relating to the underlying deal risk and use this to trade on other deal terms. Such buyers can also choose to seek a pro-sandbagging provision, which explicitly provides that the buyer's right to seek indemnification for the breach of a covered rep will not be affected by the buyer's prior knowledge of the reps' inaccuracy or breach. As a result of this possible outcome, often sellers do not even want to raise the topic of putting an anti-sandbagging provision in place unless the facts of the target business and potential deal risk give rise to such concerns of sandbagging.

When the topic of sandbagging does arise, parties can have heated negotiations where the seller may have to balance many different deal risk protections against each other. In such a balancing act, a seller could have to agree to a pro-sandbagging provision insisted on by an aggressive buyer to preserve other deal risk protections that were hard won, such as the cap on the indemnification amount or prevention of a second indemnification escrow where the buyer wants to withhold more of the purchase price at closing.

As a result, it is important for you as a founder of a start-up selling your company to understand what happens if the definitive agreement is silent on sandbagging altogether. What if you never bring up anti-sandbagging, thereby not risking a pro-sandbagging position as a possible outcome, and the buyer attempts to sandbag you post-closing?

If the definitive agreement in an M&A is silent on sandbagging, the state law governing that agreement determines whether sandbagging is permitted.

Delaware, which is our main jurisdiction of discussion in this book, is a pro-sandbagging state. So, if Delaware law governs your merger agreement, sandbagging is permitted unless the merger agreement expressly includes an anti-sandbagging provision. In contrast, California is an anti-sandbagging state such that sandbagging is not permitted unless there is an express pro-sandbagging provision. New York state law is middling – the buyer's right to sandbag the seller is contingent on how the buyer obtained its knowledge before closing that the seller is in breach of the rep the buyer is basing its indemnification claims on. If the seller disclosed the true facts to the buyer itself, then the buyer cannot maintain a claim for breach of the rep. However, if the buyer learned the true facts from a third party, not the seller, or if the true facts are common knowledge, then the buyer can still maintain a claim for breach of the rep. For me, the divergence in state law between the leading states governing contract law (and thereby laws affecting merger agreements) reflects the conflicting positions parties have about sandbagging.

In a market standards survey from 2021 by LexisNexis of 216 private company targets acquired by public companies with a deal value of $100 million or more, 125 of the deals (58 percent) were silent with regards to sandbagging, while 10 deals (5 percent) included anti-sandbagging provisions, and 81 deals (37 percent) included pro-sandbagging provisions. Of those 125 surveyed deals that did not include a sandbagging provision, most were governed by Delaware law. I am highly skeptical in using this information as "market standard" when negotiating sandbagging, especially since it does not represent private-private M&A transactions or small to lower-middle-market M&A deals. The information is also likely heavily influenced by M&A market conditions in 2021. Regardless of market trends, parties to an M&A will have to grapple with sandbagging for their particular deal.

I am pleased to end my discussion on representations and warranties, their qualifications, and attendant disclosure schedules with a primer on sandbagging. This should demonstrate to you the many and varied concepts in a private company M&A that interlace with each other in a complex (yet fascinating) way to distribute deal risk between the buyer and seller in an M&A. The final concept that I want to leave you with when thinking of deal risk in an M&A is the use of representations and warranties issuance (RWI) as an alternative, or more often as a complement, to contractual provisions like indemnification in addressing and mitigating deal risk.

REPRESENTATION AND WARRANTY INSURANCE (RWI)

Though RWI has been around since the 1990s, it has recently caught on in the M&A industry and is a common consideration now in most deals. This is a relatively new development in the M&A industry that helps both buyers and sellers reach a more amenable risk-allocation strategy in a deal when the parties are unwilling or unable to agree on the risk allocation. This type of insurance can benefit both the buyer and seller.

> **Buyers or sellers (or both) may obtain RWI to shift some of the deal risk to an insurer in exchange for payment of the policy premium. RWI provides coverage losses resulting from unknown breaches of a seller's representations and warranties in the merger agreement.**

When a buyer obtains RWI, it's a "buy-side" policy, and when a seller obtains RWI, it's a "sell-side policy."

A key concern in whether parties can avail RWI is the cost of obtaining the policy. RWI insurance is most suitable for deals with transaction values between $20 million and $2 billion and is most often utilized in deals with transaction values between $50 million and $500 million due to pricing constraints. RWI can be an expensive transaction expense and eat away at a seller's take-home purchase price. However, given increased market demands, over time some insurers are offering coverage for smaller deals lower than this threshold indicated. Deals valued over $1 billion may require coverage that exceeds most insurers' appetite for risk, although insurer pools and excess coverage policies may be available to cover these larger transactions.

Another concern in using RWI in an M&A is the scope of coverage provided by such a policy. The scope of coverage can have one or more limits on the amount the policy will pay out in US dollars after the occurrence of a covered event and also limits the nature of items that the policy will cover.

The cap or limit on the amount covered by a RWI policy depends on which party obtains the policy. In sell-side policies, the coverage limits usually equal the indemnification cap. Indemnification caps frequently range between 5 percent and 15 percent of the purchase price for breaches of most nonfundamental representations and warranties. For buy-side policies, the coverage limits usually are greater than the indemnification cap (and oftentimes are substantially greater). The coverage limits for nonfundamental representations and warranties frequently range between 10 percent and 15 percent (or 15 percent and up for smaller transactions) of the target enterprise value. Policy premiums vary and are deal specific, but premium amounts generally range between 2 percent and 4 percent of the coverage amount, typically with premiums for smaller transactions being on the higher end of the range. Buy-side policies generally tend to have higher premiums as compared to sell-side policies. Insurers often charge a minimum premium (amounts between $100,000 and $300,000 are common). For smaller transactions, the cost of RWI may be prohibitive.

RWI is generally meant to cover breaches of all general and fundamental reps within a merger agreement (e.g., misstated financials, unknown third-party claims over intellectual property, failure to obtain environmental permits, etc.), which are unknown at the time of execution of the agreement.

Additionally, preclosing tax indemnities are generally covered, but only to the extent the seller's financials are incorrectly calculated in regard to such taxes, not for failure to collect from the seller. Finally, and most importantly, a typical buy-side policy does provide buyer with the benefit of coverage for seller's fraud.

A handful of items are uniformly excluded under a typical RWI policy in the United States. These common exclusions include the following: breaches of which a member of the deal team had actual knowledge before the inception of the policy; any items listed on the seller's disclosure schedules; purchase price, working capital, or other similar post-closing adjustments (assuming none were a direct result of a breach); breaches relating to covenants or post-closing statements; contingent claims based on future events (such as, a promise to indemnify a buyer against potential antitrust claims); or failure to meet financial projections and other forward-looking statements.

It is important to keep in mind that insurers will not cover *known* risks or liabilities in a deal. However, buy-side policies generally cover undisclosed breaches that may be known only by the seller and not disclosed. Sell-side policies may distinguish among sellers that have different degrees of knowledge (for example, management's knowledge of a breach may not necessarily preclude recovery by an unaware institutional seller). However, even if RWI policies do not cover known risks and liabilities, there may be other insurance products available for these specific types of risks. Some of these uniquely insured risks can include Fair Labor Standards Act violations, environmental or pollution cleanup and other environmental liabilities, Foreign Corrupt Practice Act violations, product liability claims, pension plan liabilities, intellectual property rights, and certain tax attributes (including deferred tax assets).

COVERING YOUR BEHIND

Whether or not to purchase sell-side RWI policy to cover your unknown deal risks during the sale of your company is a business decision for you to consider. Now you can make this decision more confidently because you understand how an RWI policy helps you cover unknown risks and liabilities and what the limits of such coverage can be. You are also now aware of how the reps you provide for your target business can be qualified to make them more accurate and complete, limiting the bases for indemnification claims after closing. You have learned key concepts that illustrate how certain risk-shifting provisions, such as anti-sandbagging, interplay with other risk-shifting provisions like indemnification for breach of reps to protect you in a deal. Together with the previous chapter, you are now as informed as any seasoned entrepreneur on how deal risk is attributed and negotiated in an M&A.

10

EXPLORING POST-CLOSING
EMPLOYMENT

When you decide to marry your partner in a traditional Christian wedding ceremony, you will exchange vows with him. This exchange of the vows is at the heart of marriage and goes something like this: "I, take thee, to be my wedded husband, to have and to hold from this day forward, for better, for worse, for richer, for poorer, in sickness and in health, to love and to cherish, till death do us part." How beautiful. How timeless.

Such wedding vows are akin to a particular type of important provisions you will encounter in an M&A – covenants. I know I mentioned in Chapter 3 when laying out a roadmap of the M&A journey for you that the analogy of dating and marriage breaks down when we arrive at the signing of the definitive agreement. It's true. Being married is nothing like entering into a business contract. Wedding vows exchanged in a marriage ceremony are emotional and spiritual and lend divine blessing to the ceremony. Entering into a definitive agreement that lays out the terms and conditions of an M&A hardly exists on the same plane as a marriage. However, similar to wedding vows, parties in an M&A will "exchange vows" – they will enter into covenants relating to how and when the parties shall consummate an M&A when they sign the merger agreement.

POST-CLOSING COVENANTS

Covenants are ongoing promises by a party to take or refrain from taking, certain actions in the future. The former are "positive covenants" while the latter are "negative covenants."

In a wedding vow, you are making the ongoing promise to have and to hold your husband until death parts you two. This is a negative covenant – it's a promise to not let go of your partner voluntarily. In a merger agreement, covenants obligate the parties to perform, or prohibit them from performing, certain acts that are meant to preserve the value of the target business and ensure that the M&A transaction is consummated according to the terms and conditions set by the parties. This chapter is an introduction to covenants in private company M&A. Recall from chapter 8 that the breach of covenants can be a basis for indemnification claims. However, unlike the breach of representations and warranties, covenants are not a monolithic concept. Due to their very nature, each covenant is independent of others.

Since covenants aim to control a party's behavior in the future, parties need to consider possible outcomes, their effects, and how to place constraint in a feasible manner. As a result, there are no standard limitations or strategies applicable to covenants as a whole. Instead, we will be discussing covenants in connection with the common concerns or future scenarios in an M&A that parties often have to address.

> **There are generally two types covenants: (1) preclosing covenants, that usually operate during the Interim Period when there is a separate signing and closing in an M&A, and (2) post-closing covenants, that usually operate after the closing of the M&A.**

In this chapter, we will explore a type of post-closing negative covenants that will likely apply to you and your start-up during a sale of your company – noncompete, nonsolicit, and nondisparagement. This type of covenant is generally referred to as "restrictive covenants" because they are promises by a party to refrain from taking certain actions that the party would have otherwise been free to take. I will discuss restrictive covenants in a private company M&A in this chapter along with a general overview of post-closing covenants. In the next chapter, I will discuss preclosing covenants and how to navigate them successfully in an M&A.

THE EXECUTIVE EMPLOYEE

In addition to, and in parallel with, the post-closing negative covenants, this chapter explores one of your many roles in an M&A as a founder selling your company. The previous chapters were written for you as the founder who is also the chief executive officer or some other key executive of the start-up. I assumed that in your role as such an active key executive, you are deeply engaged in the vision and execution of the M&A. That's why you needed to know the high-value and high-impact concepts in an M&A that I have covered in prior chapters. In this chapter, I focus on your role as an executive employee of the target company. In Chapter 11, when providing a primer on the fiduciary duties of the board of directors of a company engaging in an M&A, I focus on your role as a director of the target company.

As a key executive employee of the target company, you may have a choice to stay on with the company post-closing.

Especially if the buyer is making a strategic acquisition where you as the founder of the target company are critical to the success of the target business post-closing, the buyer may offer you a job to stay on with your company and work for the buyer. For some M&As, the acquisition of the team or talent is the main goal to drive business synergies – those deals are referred to as "acquihires." For successful founders, this opportunity to continue after an M&A can be the ideal outcome. If both preparation and opportunity meet for you, your efforts resulted in a high company valuation where your share of the take-home purchase price as a stockholder in the target company is already a fortune. As a key executive, you negotiated the terms of the M&A based on the directions from the target company's board of directors to maximize the value of the M&A for stockholders of the target company. More on this part of the story in Chapter 12. In so doing, you have also maximized your own share of the take-home purchase price as a stockholder.

If you have this choice, what will you do?

After working for yourself all these years quite success-fully, do you want to work for someone else now? Are you ready to retire (early)? Do you just want to get on a one-way flight to an island paradise of your dreams and think about all of this later? Or just rest and recover for a while? Do you want to spend some quality time with friends and family you have ignored all these years to painfully climb this tall, steep ladder? It's a hard choice.

Often, a strategic buyer will therefore make its offer to purchase a target company contingent upon the continued employment of one or more key executive employees post-closing.

Key executives like you who know the secret sauce, and certain buyers see their continued employment and service as indispensable to preserve the value of the company they bought and to realize the expected business synergies.

Executive Employee Compensation

Even if you agree to stay, there is no guarantee you will work hard enough to realize the buyer's expected business synergies from the M&A.

This is what the buyer will argue when they seek to negotiate your post-closing executive compensation terms in a manner that aligns your compensative incentives with the buyer's business goals for the target.

The terms will have to be sweet enough to make you delay for one to five years – or maybe even indefinitely – your retirement or reward from successfully selling your company. This is an opportunity for you as a founder to secure a generous executive compensation offer. Often, you don't have to do much extra work for it. It just so happens that a larger acquirer's standard compensation package for its executive employees, like the salary of a CEO heading a key business division of a public, multinational conglomerate, is much higher than the standard compensation package of a small or midsize private company, like your salary as the CEO of the start-up.

However, if your buyer is not a public company who often discloses the compensation terms for its key executive officers, then the negotiation to secure an adequate executive compensation package is a heated one. Additionally, your business may not be selling for a value high enough to make you a fortune in purchase price proceeds or executive compensation. This is an incredibly difficult success metric to achieve, so be kind to yourself as you read this chapter.

In most merger scenarios, the vast majority of employees do not receive such retention packages – typically, less than 2 percent of the target business employees should receive such incentives. However, those few critical employees need to be identified quickly. They could have highly specialized and hard-to-access skills or knowledge vital to running the surviving company (such as expertise in the legacy IT systems). They may be important for ensuring stability during the integration phase or they may be high performers essential to building the next phase of the surviving company. These are often referred to as "key employees." A buyer may require that certain named key employees remain employed by the target company at the time of the closing of the transaction and make that a closing condition. We discuss closing conditions in the next chapter.

COVENANTS OF THE SURVIVING COMPANY

There are a number of different post-closing covenants that can bind a surviving company (the company that survives after the merger) or an executive employee. Here, I illustrate two covenants that often bind a surviving company: (1) the provision and maintenance of certain benefit arrangements for the target's employees and the (2) maintenance of insurance for the target's directors & officers. In the following section, I discuss the covenants that typically bind executive employees – called restrictive covenants.

There are, of course, many other types of post-closing covenants that could apply, such as a covenant that required each party to take any further actions necessary or desirable to consummate the M&A post-closing (often seen in asset sales) or a covenant that lays out the tax treatment of the M&A in each party's tax reporting. We cannot go into each covenant here. However, we focus on particular covenants that could be important to you as a founder of the target business.

Employee Benefits

One of my memorable M&A deals involved the thorny negotiation of a post-closing employee benefit covenant. The founder of the start-up being sold was expecting his first baby. His wife was pregnant after years of trying, and it was a complicated medical situation. The large, public company buyer wanted the start-up to terminate all its health insurance benefits so all the start-up employees staying on would move to the buyer's health insurance, which was a lot better. However, the founder's wife couldn't accept this. She needed to continue the existing healthcare coverage to maintain her current specialized healthcare team. This led to some phone-tag negotiations where I couldn't divulge any private health information but had to convince the buyer and its many advisors and vendors there was good reason for them to accommodate our request. Ultimately, we were able to convince the relevant parties, their legal and employment advisers, and their various respective health insurance brokers and administrators to put in place a customized covenant binding both buyer and seller. The custom covenant respected the buyer's uniform health benefits administration for all employees but also allowed a feasible workaround for the founder's wife to maintain her coverage. We closed that deal. This experience highlights for me the need for covenants to be drafted to fit the unique promises parties are seeking.

Generally, the covenants addressing employment benefits for the target business's employees depend on several business considerations. Will the buyer employ some or all of the target business' employees? If it does, will those compensation packages be better or worse than what the employees have now? Will some employees be let go at or after the closing, and are they entitled to severance? Which party should bear the respective costs? Often, the buyer and seller will have to collaborate to determine how to proceed with each employee and service provider (in groups or subgroups, individually or in any other manner that makes sense). A key part of such determination is whether some or all employees will continue post-closing, and if they do continue, what their compensation will be. Sometimes the buyer has existing employment compensation parameters, and the target company's continuing employees will be placed within that schema. In some cases, the buyer and seller will work together to craft nonstandard compensation packages for key employees – often executives.

D&O Insurance

Directors and officers (D&O) insurance (DOI) is an important risk mitigating option for you as a key executive negotiating the M&A deal. This is a type of liability insurance that protects the D&O of a company from personal losses if they are sued for wrongful acts while managing the company.

In the context of M&A, directors and officers insurance become particularly important because directors and officers can face lawsuits from stockholders, employees, buyer or other third parties alleging breaches of fiduciary duties or other wrongful acts like fraud related to the M&A transaction.

This insurance covers legal fees, settlements, and other costs associated with defending against such claims. D&O "tail" insurance, also known as "runoff" coverage, extends the D&O insurance policy for a specified period after the company's sale if it already has D&O liability insurance in place.

In a transaction where the target business's D&O will not be continuing their service following the closing, the seller may ask the buyer to maintain D&O liability insurance coverage for such persons post-closing for a set period of time (usually six years). The buyer may seek to cap the premium it is required to pay. Because insurance premiums can change over time, the seller should price the coverage before agreeing to a cap. For a "tail" insurance policy, seller can price it as a percentage of the existing annual premium and purchase the policy in full at the closing as transaction expense and thus avoid reliance on the buyer to maintain post-closing coverage. The cost of D&O tail insurance for three to six years post-closing depends on many factors but is usually around 250 percent of the annual premium. In the last couple of years, the cost of tail coverage has increased significantly, with some options exceeding 300 percent of the annual premium.

RESTRICTIVE COVENANTS

The buyer in an M&A transaction may seek to include various protective measures to limit the seller's ability to compete with or otherwise disrupt the target business once the transaction has closed. Such measures, which may be addressed in the definitive agreement or in one or more ancillary agreements, include:

1. noncompetition, which prevents a seller from competing with the business of the target;
2. nonsolicitation, which prevents a seller from soliciting or hiring key target personnel in order to establish a competing business;
3. nondisparagement, which prevents a seller from harming the target's reputation; and
4. confidentiality, which prevents a seller from disclosing sensitive information acquired during its ownership of the target's business and prohibits the use of such information in a competing business.

I dig a little deeper into noncompetes and nonsolicits but largely rely on this general description of nondisparagement and confidentiality obligations.

Noncompete

A noncompete arrangement typically stems from one of two types of relationships between the parties: an employer-employee relationship and a seller-buyer relationship.

Employer-Employee Noncompete

A new US Federal Trade Commission (FTC) regulation sought to ban most employer-employee noncompetes, subject to exceptions. The rule bans noncompetes nationwide, protecting the fundamental freedom of workers to change jobs, increasing innovation, and foster new business formation. This rule was supposed to be effective after August 2024. The Northern District of Texas in *Ryan LLC v. Federal Trade Commission* issued a nationwide injunction, effectively blocking the FTC's rule from taking effect on September 4, 2024. The judge concluded that the FTC exceeded its statutory authority in implementing the rule, as the agency lacks substantive rulemaking authority with respect to unfair methods of competition. Additionally, the rule was deemed arbitrary and capricious because it was unreasonably overbroad without a reasonable explanation. As a result, employers are not required to comply with the rule's notice and other requirements. The FTC is considering an appeal, so the situation may evolve. Notably, the final rule that is now suspended does *not* exempt executives and other highly compensated employees with policymaking authority and total annual compensation of at least $151,164 from the noncompete ban, though it does permit the enforcement of existing noncompetes with such individuals.

Seller-Buyer Relationship

The final rule that is now suspended provides a broad exception for any noncompete entered into pursuant to a bona fide sale of a business in an M&A.

In a seller-buyer relationship, noncompetes are thriving. This type of noncompete forms part of the consideration offered by the seller to induce the buyer to acquire the target in the M&A transaction. An individual such as yourself, as a founder selling your company, may be subject to both types of noncompete provisions, both as an employee and as a seller. The enforceability of a noncompete can differ depending on whether it is employment-based or transaction-based, and depending on the applicable jurisdiction. For example, California prohibits noncompetition measures tied to an individual's employment, deeming them illegal restraints on trade, but permits them when the noncompete is tied to the sale of a stockholder's interests in a business (even when not in connection with an M&A). Consistent with the sale of a business exception in the FTC's noncompete ban, sale of business noncompetes are generally viewed more favorably by courts – and thus are more likely enforceable – across all jurisdictions.

In the context of an M&A transaction, the buyer will likely ask for a covenant or agreement prohibiting the sellers or stockholders from competing with the acquired business. Buyers ask for noncompetes to protect the value of the business they are acquiring from customer poaching, leveraging existing know-how, and other tactics that sellers may take through a competing enterprise. A noncompetition obligation will typically only take effect if and when the M&A transaction closes. A noncompete should address, among other things, the applicable law or jurisdiction; the definition of the competitive activity being prohibited; the geographic scope of the noncompete; duration of the noncompete; and any other key concerns of those bound by it.

NONSOLICIT

A prohibition on the seller's solicitation of the target business's employees may be included for two reasons. First, as with the noncompetition covenant, the value of the acquired business could be compromised if the seller hires the target's employees. Second, if the M&A transaction does not close, each party may still want to prevent the other from poaching its employees, especially if the parties are competitors. It is for this second reason that nonsolicitation measures are typically effective upon the signing of the merger agreement and, unlike noncompetition measures, are not conditioned on the closing of the M&A.

A nonsolicitation covenant generally provides that each party will not solicit for employment or hire the other party's employees for some period of time (generally shorter than the noncompete, often applying for one to two years following closing). A signatory to such an arrangement may still generally hire the other party's employees – it just cannot solicit the hiring of such employees. For example, there are usually exceptions permitting the hiring of employees: (1) through general, untargeted advertisements or (2) who approach the nonsolicit bound party of their own accord, without any prohibited solicitation or inducement by the bound party.

A nonsolicit can also prevent a seller from soliciting the target business' customer, in which case the provision is a form of noncompete. In addition to restrictive covenants, as an executive employee, you will also have to negotiate compensation terms, which I discuss next.

Being Restricted in California

The negotiation of restrictive covenants for founders focuses on the enforcement of post-closing restrictive covenants, such as noncompete and nonsolicitation clauses. Here, a case study from California (where employer-employee covenants are banned) is illustrative of how local employment law affects the employment compensation terms.

PacWest Bancorp sued its former executives, including David I. Rainer, for allegedly violating their M&A related post-closing covenants by joining a competitor, Bank of Southern California N.A. (SoCal Bank) and soliciting PacWest employees to leave.[1]

PacWest claimed that Rainer and others breached their employment agreements by soliciting employees during the restricted period outlined in their contracts. Though California law generally voids noncompete clauses under Business and Professions Code section 16600, courts will enforce covenants that protect confidential information, such as employee data, from being used for competitive purposes.

PacWest also accused the defendants of using trade secrets—specifically salary and employee performance data—to recruit employees to SoCal Bank. The court found that some of PacWest's claims were preempted by the California Uniform Trade Secrets Act (CUTSA) because they arose

---

1. *PacWest Bancorp v. David I. Rainer*, decided by the Superior Court of California in 2022. PacWest Bancorp entered into employment contracts with several senior executives, including David I. Rainer, Richard Hernandez, and Diana Remington Smithson (the "Individual Defendants"), in connection with an M&A. As part of these agreements, the executives were bound by restrictive covenants, which included noncompete and nonsolicitation provisions, designed to prevent them from working for competitors or poaching employees for a set period after they left the company.

from the same facts as the trade secret misappropriation claims. However, the court allowed other claims, including intentional interference with contractual relations, to proceed.

The court held that nonsolicitation clauses could be enforceable if they protect trade secrets or confidential information. It also acknowledged that defendants' actions during the restricted period, such as soliciting employees using PacWest's proprietary information, could constitute unfair competition.

While noncompete clauses are limited in California, founders must still respect confidentiality and nonsolicitation agreements, especially if they involve trade secrets. Enforcement of a noncompete can be a remedy to misusing employer data or proprietary information post-closing. The legal consequences of violating post-closing obligations can result in lawsuits for breach of contract, trade secret misappropriation, and unfair competition.

INCENTIVE COMPENSATION

In addition to a cash base salary, and possibly also a cash bonus, much of the complexity around crafting executive compensation for a key employee in an M&A is the noncash incentive compensation to be granted by the buyer. If the key employee has existing equity compensation awards from the target company at the time of closing the M&A – which most invariably do – it creates an additional layer of complexity. In crafting the right incentive package, the buyer will take its que from the existing compensation awards for the key employee and weave that into the crafting of the new package. In this section, I discuss generally the type of such equity awards and how they may be addressed in an M&A so you are better informed when it comes to negotiating your package.

Grant of Equity

Most key employees in a private company, especially the founder, hold a substantial amount of stock or options in the target company at the time of closing an M&A.

Stock is the direct ownership in the company, represented by the number of shares held by a stockholder. An option is the right to purchase a certain number of shares of stock in the private company at a pre-fixed price called the strike price.

Options are usually granted to service providers to the company as part of their compensation: the strike price reflects the current valuation at the time of the grant of the option and the hope is that when the service provider's option vests and she exercises the option to purchase the underlying shares, the strike price will be much lower than the fair market value of those shares so the service provider will gain the difference. Founders often receive restricted common stock in the private company at the time of founding. Then over time, founders may receive additional grants of more restricted common stock or options to maintain their owner-ship stake as more equity holders dilute the cap table.

Vesting

The grant of such stock or option is restricted because private company stock cannot be freely sold without complying with securities laws and applicable exemptions. Recall our discussion from earlier chapters like Chapters 4 and 6. Additionally, all or part of the grant of stock or options can be subject to a vesting schedule, where the unvested portion of the grant is subject to forfeiture (or other right of repurchase) if the founder is terminated for cause or good reason. The standard vesting schedule of options granted by start-ups to their employees is a four-year vesting term where 25 percent of the shares subject to the options vest at the one-year anniversary of the grant date, often called a one-year cliff, and then the remainder vests pro rata each month for the remaining three years.

Acceleration

One aspect of the vesting terms is whether there is acceleration of vesting upon a specified event, such as a change of control event like an M&A. Recently, the trend is for key employees to have equity grants be subject to double-trigger vesting benefits for long-term stock (or options). Grants of equity that provide for automatic acceleration of vesting upon a change in control event like an M&A are referred to as "single-trigger acceleration awards," while grants that provide for automatic vesting only on an involuntary termination without "cause" (or a "good reason" termination) within a specified period before or following a change in control event like an M&A are referred to as "double-trigger acceleration awards."

There are two general treatments for such equity compensation awards during an M&A. The portion of the awards that have vested often receive consideration from the deal. The portion of the awards that have not vested or,

in the case of options, that have also vested but not been exercised by the holder can be cashed out or rollover over.

Cash-Out

Where equity compensation awards are cashed out, the holders normally receive the excess, if any, of the per share purchase price of the share award over the strike price in exchange for the canceling of the award at the closing. Payment is made by the buyer in cash. Cashing out awards is administratively convenient for the buyer because the award is gone. Cashing out awards also aligns the interests between the stockholders and executives by treating them similarly in an all-cash consideration M&A. In addition, cashing out may be preferable to rolling over in cases where the buyer determines that the buyer's stock awards are not as attractive to the executives as the target company's awards because the executives don't have the same potential to affect the value of buyer's stock as they did the target company's stock.

Underwater Awards

One complicating issue is dealing with underwater options. If a company's valuation falls after the grant of the option such that the strike price is lower than the fair market value of the shares at the time of exercise, the option is "underwater." Often, depending on the terms of the equity plan or option agreement for that grant, such underwater options are canceled without any consideration. Most equity plans and option agreements are now drafted to clearly permit the plan administrator to cancel underwater awards for no consideration without the option holder's consent. However, where neither the equity plan document nor the award agreement provides such authority to the plan administrator, Delaware courts have recently held that the award holder is entitled to the economic value of their awards. As a founder, you should make sure your equity plan administrator – often the board of directors of your start-up – have the explicit authority to cancel underwater awards. This can significantly help in the event you have to sell your company.

Rollover

Rather than cashing out equity incentive awards, the buyer in an M&A may want to roll over awards by assuming the awards and the seller's equity plan(s) or by assuming the awards into an equity plan of the buyer (new or existing).

Any of these is considered a "rollover." If this is done, the buyer's stock will be used to settle the awards generally in accordance with their original terms. The rollover of awards reflects a different incentive mechanism from cash-outs. For example, the rollover of unvested awards may reflect a viewpoint that a cash-out by reason of a change in control is inappropriate as a governance matter because it represents a windfall to management. Some target company executives may view a cash-out as inappropriate because of the diminished value of unvested awards by terminating them prior to the expiration of their terms. Moreover, options are sometimes rolled over where the target company has not reserved the contractual right to cash out the options and a large number of options are underwater at the transaction price per share. However, where outstanding equity awards are assumed, the buyer's shares used for insurance, exercise, or settlement of the assumed awards are not offset against the purchaser's existing equity incentive pool of shares.

Many buyers do not want to assume outstanding equity awards unless the awards have significant retention value, or the buyer wants to manage dilution under its own equity plan(s). As a result, you should consider allowing a buyer to assume equity awards when advantageous to do so, subject to any requirements provided in the target company's equity plan(s) and award agreements and accelerating all or a portion of the unvested awards for a cash-out when the buyer elects not to assume outstanding awards. This approach provides flexibility to the buyer and assures executives and other affected employees that all their unvested awards will not terminate upon a change of control for no value.

Once you have set up the executive compensation package with the proper incentive mechanism from equity awards, you should consider whether executives are being such a high amount in an M&A that it could trigger 280G concerns, which I discuss next.

GET YOUR OWN LAWYER

Part of the executive compensation package you will be offered by a buyer who wants to employ you post-closing will include restrictive covenants, such as noncompetes, nonsolic-its, nondisparagement, and confidentiality obligations. In addition to such restrictive covenants, you will also be negoti-ating your base salary, any contingent or deferred pay, any bonuses, and the benefits and leave conditions. This is akin to negotiating any high-stakes job offer.

One of the important decisions to make here is whether you should hire your own lawyer to advise you on the executive compensation package offered by the buyer. Your M&A lawyer primarily represents the target company in the deal. As a founder who is a major stockholder and also a key executive, you have to negotiate numerous deal terms that directly affect your individual interests while negotiating the deal terms at large – and from a buyer's perspective these two parallel negotiations feed off each other in crafting the deal as a whole. So, when you are negotiating the post-closing terms for yourself like base salary, incentive compensation and bonuses in parallel with M&A deal terms like purchase price adjustments and risk-shifting indemnification, these parallel responsibilities can give rise to conflicts of interest between your individual interests as an individual and the target company's and stockholders' interests in the M&A.

In such a scenario, it may be highly advisable for you to engage your own executive employment lawyer to advise you (and maybe other similarly situated executives at the same time) separately from the M&A lawyer who is representing the target company. What the extent of the potential conflicts of interest are and whether those can be waived by you and the target company to be represented by the same M&A lawyer depends on the facts of your deal – and budget. However, some of the best sell-side M&A lawyers I know advise their clients to get their own executive employment counsel as a rule, recognizing that this is a critical financial decision for you and your counsel should be unencumbered with conflicting interests. While it may add to the transaction costs and add more members to the deal team to keep abreast, you would be doing yourself a disservice if you are not availing this option if and when you can.

In addition to your own executive compensation lawyer who will help you negotiate your post-closing employment (or separation) terms, you should also consider hiring an estate planning and tax attorney for yourself prior to signing the M&A deal – especially if you stand to make a lot of money. Many founders or executives in this situation wait until the M&A deal has been completed before reaching out to an estate planner or tax advisor, but I strongly prefer to advise my clients to consider getting this counsel before you sign on the virtual dotted line. While your M&A lawyer will likely tell you what the general tax consequences of the deal terms would be on the stockholders as a group, they are not aware of your particular financial situation and cannot tailor advice to you. Especially if part of the deal consideration is stock or seller financing, it's important to understand what the tax landscape looks for you before you agree to the deal terms.

THE BUSINESS VOWS

In this chapter I introduced you to a few post-closing covenants that could have a big impact on the proceeds you receive or the risk you carry in a transaction, such as whether to purchase D&O insurance. In this chapter I also aimed to address some key concepts that relate specifically to you as an executive employee of a target company in an M&A: the post-closing restrictive covenants you will have to negotiate for the sellers or stockholders in parallel with the same covenants that you may have to negotiate for yourself as an employee. In so doing, I warned you about the risk of using the same M&A lawyer as the target company due to potential conflicts.

11

SUCCESSFULLY CLOSING AN M&A

W e are so close to the finish line you can now taste victory. It is simultaneously and quite intensely nerve-racking and exhilarating to work through this stage of the M&A process. This is the stage of the deal where the unique personalities of the individuals involved in the M&A reveal themselves. Everyone handles stress differently and at this stage, with the finish line so close yet illusive, the stress can be palpable.

Each person's approach to handling stress becomes evident. It is less frequent nowadays, but there are still some people who do not handle stress well, or professionally. Once, a founder got so angry when I was giving him the present vote count of the stockholders' approval of the deal that he yelled at me for a few minutes until he stopped abruptly; I later found out from his secretary he had thrown his cell phone into the pool. Another time, the entire M&A team received an unacceptable email from a venture fund stockholder of the target company who held their approval hostage until my employer firm reduced their significant – yet at that time, undeterminable – legal bill. Then one other time the founder of a target company and I were both awake at 2:00 a.m. waiting on some stockholders in a distant, foreign land to deliver their vote to meet the final closing condition, and we kept each other awake by exchanging stories about horrible people we had done business with. That founder later sent me an amazing gift basket of baked goods from his local bakery in Michigan. This period before closing is an emotional time.

For M&A practitioners like me, we push and pull each of our clients to reach this significant milestone of closing a deal – which, for some, can generate life-altering wealth. I aim to match the emotional intensity my founders bring to the transaction. For me, it's like attending one best friend's wedding after another and catering to each bride's needs as they see fit. Part of my responsibility as the bridesmaid in an M&A is to make sure that the closing goes off without a hitch. Much like a wedding, there are many people to coordinate and tasks to complete to bring about a successful closing. In order to do this, I begin preparation for closing early and anticipate every little thing that could get out of control, or go wrong, and try to get rid of it or minimize it. This is where closing conditions in an M&A are critical. Until you meet all the closing conditions applicable to you, the buyer is not obligated to close the deal. I talk about some of the high-impact closing conditions in this chapter.

I also continue our exploration of covenants here. As previewed, I discuss preclosing covenants that operate during the Interim Period between signing and closing. Often, like in the case of a 280G stockholder vote, an affirmative preclosing covenant relates to one or more closing conditions that a party must fulfil to be able to close the M&A. In order to make your reading more fluid, I will group the key preclosing covenants with their attendant closing condition and discuss the concept as a whole.

PRECLOSING COVENANTS

There are three types of preclosing covenants: (1) those that relate to the operation of the business, (2) those that facilitate closing, and (3) those that govern the relationship of the seller and other potential buyers. For this first type, the seller's preclosing covenants will always be more onerous than the buyer's covenants because they concern the business, or assets, being sold.

These preclosing covenants are seller's obligations to maintain the status quo and the value of the business during the period between the signing and closing – the Interim Period.

If the buyer will deliver its equity securities as consideration in the deal, then the buyer's preclosing covenants may also include obligations to maintain the status quo and value of such securities during the Interim Period between the signing and closing.

Let's briefly focus on the first type of preclosing covenants – those that relate to the seller's operation of the business. Most often, sellers find this covenant innocuous and reasonable. However, given the nature of covenants – that they are ongoing promises about an unknown future – it is critical to ensure that as a seller you are able to comply with the covenant to the letter. The proposed acquisition of AB Stable VIII LLC by Maps Hotels & Resorts One LLC (both private companies) was not consummated because the buyer successfully proved in litigation that the seller breached its preclosing covenant because of changes the seller had to make in its business in response to the COVID-19 pandemic. The definitive acquisition agreement mandated the seller to operate "only in the ordinary course of business, consistent with past practice in all material respects." The seller then closed down hotels and reduced staff, which was inconsistent with its past practice but was reasonable and consistent with industry practices during the pandemic. However, the court looked to the text of the covenant only and noted that the covenant required seller to be consistent with its own operational history. Since this decision by the Delaware Supreme Court in 2021, sellers are more vigilant and they seek to ensure that the preclosing covenant governing conduct of the business is qualified by a "commercially reasonable efforts," "best efforts," or some other reasonableness standard.

There are a number of pre-closing covenants that relate to the seller's operation of the business during the Interim Period that are often negotiated and included in a definitive agreement. According to the 2023 ABA M&A Deal Points Study, 60 percent of the deals surveyed included a covenant of the seller to notify the buyer in the event the target discovered a breach of its reps. 100 percent of the deals surveyed included the covenant to operate the business in its ordinary course, which I just discussed.

The second type of preclosing covenants that seek to facilitate the closing obligate both parties to take certain actions in furtherance of closing the transaction, such as obtaining necessary approvals and complying with regulatory requirements.

One popular preclosing covenant here relates to the

parties' obligations under antitrust laws and governmental approval under such laws as the closing condition for the deal.

M&As are primarily governed by Section 7 of the Clayton Act, which prohibits transactions that may substantially lessen competition or tend to create a monopoly. This section applies broadly to acquisitions of stock or assets and includes the formation of joint ventures. The Hart-Scott-Rodino Antitrust Improvements Act (the HSR Act), as amended, further strengthens enforcement by requiring premerger notifications to the Federal Trade Commission (FTC) and the Antitrust Division of the Justice Department, allowing these agencies to investigate M&A transactions before they close. The antitrust review process involves evaluating the potential anticompetitive effects of mergers, such as market share dominance, reduced competition, and increased entry barriers. The FTC and the Antitrust Division have the authority to enjoin (or stop) transactions that are likely to reduce competition substantially.

The HSR Act applies to transactions that exceed certain size-of-transaction and size-of-party thresholds – and this analysis is conducted by lawyers or economists who specialize in antitrust rules. As of the most recent adjustments, the base filing threshold for reporting is $101 million. This means that if the value of the M&A exceeds $101 million, the parties involved must file a notification with the FTC and DOJ. If the transaction involves the acquisition of voting securities or assets valued over $359.9 million, it is subject to HSR filing requirements regardless of the size of the parties involved. The time for review by the authorities upon filing usually takes at least thirty days, sometimes more or less, and this waiting period falls within the Interim Period.

Antitrust enforcement actions under the Biden-Harris

administration and in the European Union have increased compared to prior decades. One prominent example is the failed acquisition of Adobe by Figma. In September 2022, Figma announced that it had entered into an agreement to be acquired by Adobe for $20 billion in cash and stock. It was a mega merger that marked the peak of technology M&A. The transaction came under significant scrutiny from antitrust regulators in the United States under the HSR Act and also in the European Union under its antitrust policy. After fifteen months of negotiations with antitrust regulators, both Figma and Adobe decided they could not structure the M&A in a manner that preserved their business goals while appeasing the antitrust regulators' concerns, so they abandoned the signed deal. The parties mutually agreed to terminate the merger agreement.

The final and third type of preclosing covenants govern the seller's ability to seek, respond to, or entertain other potential buyers during the preclosing period. In Chapter 3, we discussed the exclusivity agreement that a potential buyer will seek to enter into before investing time and resources on diligence or negotiation. Often in an M&A, the buyer will push to agree on the deal terms and sign the merger agreement before the exclusivity period expires. Once the parties sign the agreement, depending on the nature of the transaction and expected length of the Interim Period, the buyer can also put in place additional covenants that extend and enhance the exclusivity arrangement. Such covenants are similar to the no-shop provisions I previously discussed. According to the 2023 ABA M&A Deal Points Study, 90 percent of the deals analyzed had some form of a no-shop covenant applicable during the Interim Period.

Since we will discuss the other key concepts in preclosing covenants together with the closing conditions, I will now introduce the concept of closing conditions and then dive into discussing some of these concepts.

CLOSING CONDITIONS

The failure to satisfy any closing condition gives a party whose obligation to close the deal is subject to the condition the right to terminate the merger agreement.

Although failure of a condition typically does not provide a right to monetary damages or indemnification (unless the parties agreed in writing), it could provide leverage to the innocent party to renegotiate deal terms in exchange for not refusing to close or terminating the agreement due to failure to satisfy the condition.

As a seller motivated to close the sale of your company, you should be allergic to closing conditions that allow the buyer to walk away from the deal through no fault of your own.

There is no limit to the closing conditions a buyer would impose on a seller. A common one is the "bringdown" of the representations and warranties. This condition requires the seller's reps to be true and correct as of the closing date (in addition to the signing date when seller entered into the definitive agreement). Another common closing condition, often mutual, is that the other party must not have experienced a material adverse effect or material adverse change (MAC/MAE), a qualifier we also discussed in Chapter 9. Instead of providing a laundry list of all the closing conditions a buyer can pin on a seller, I will highlight some high-impact conditions here that sellers often have to struggle with to successfully close an M&A. However, please bear in mind that there are many other pre-losing covenants and closing conditions I won't be able to discuss here.

Buyer Financing

If the buyer needs to obtain financing from a third-party in order to make the acquisition, this could be a critical preclosing covenant that facilitates the closing. A buyer in such a scenario will want its financing to be a closing condition and the seller will insist on putting in place a financing covenant that specifies the steps the buyer must take, and the level of effort it must exert, to obtain the financing promptly. A financing closing condition without a financing preclosing covenant will just allow the buyer to simply walk away from closing the deal by willfully failing to obtain the financing. Importantly, the seller should also require the buyer to indemnify it for any actions taken in connection with the financing and to reimburse the target business for any fees and expenses it incurs in connection with the financing. In such a scenario, a financing covenant can be coupled with a termination fee – which is another type of preclosing covenant that might come into play if a party fails to consummate the M&A.

Termination Fees

Most merger agreements contain certain termination provisions that allow one or more parties to terminate the merger agreement and abandon the transaction prior to closing. For example, either party may terminate the agreement in the event that any court of competent jurisdiction or other governmental body issues an order, or takes any other action, prohibiting the transactions. Another standard provision in definitive agreements provide each party a termination right in the event the other party breaches or fails to perform any of its representations, warranties, or covenants; such provision may allow for a cure period of twenty to forty-five days following notice to the defaulting party of the breach or failure to perform.

Termination fees are usually provided for in public target transactions to compensate the buyer for the effort it has put into its attempted acquisition of the target business and to provide some comfort to the buyer that there will be reasonable deterrents in place to thwart competing bidders once the deal is announced. Private transactions typically do not include termination fees because (1) private transactions tend to be locked up to a much greater degree than public transactions and, (2) typically, there is not enough publicly available information about the private target that a third party can use to make a credible competing offer without significant conditions.

Like termination fees, reverse break-up fees are typically a feature of public company transactions but are occasionally, though rarely, used in private deals to address a seller's concerns about a buyer's incentives for closing the deal (for example, they may be used in place of a hell-or-high-water efforts standard to incentivize a buyer to dispose of certain assets in order to obtain regulatory approval) or to serve as liquidated damages and a cap on a buyer's liability in connection with the failure to obtain financing.

Unlike a standard termination fee, which is paid by the target business to the buyer, a reverse break-up fee is paid by the buyer to the

target business in the event that the transaction does not close due to the buyer's breach or failure to perform.

Termination rights, and any corresponding fees payable at termination, are highly negotiated provisions – the seller or target company is typically balancing the desire for certainty of closing with the flexibility to exit the transaction if a superior proposal comes along or if circumstances materially change so that it can honor its fiduciary duties. The buyer is seeking to preserve the transaction while also maximizing its own flexibility if circumstances change in a way that adversely affects the deal or the value of the target company to the buyer's detriment.

Termination fees in private company M&A involving Delaware private corporations are generally considered reasonable if they fall within a certain percentage of the transaction or equity value. They have often been the subject of stockholder litigation, so case law is pretty substantial on this topic. Delaware courts have consistently upheld termination fees that are around 3 percent of the equity or transaction value. The reasonableness of termination fees is often evaluated based on the specific facts surrounding the transaction. For example, in *In re Smurfit-Stone Container Corp. S'holder Litig.*, a termination fee of approximately 3.4 percent of the equity value was considered to be at the upper boundary of permissibility but still within the range of reasonableness due to the reciprocal nature of the fee and the good faith, arm's-length negotiations involved.

It is also important to note that the preclusive effect of a termination fee is measured by its impact on potential bidders. In *In re Dollar Thrifty S'holder Litig.*, the Delaware court highlighted that the preclusive aspect of a termination fee should be assessed based on how it affects the desire of any potential bidder to make a topping bid. This perspective ensures that termination fees do not unduly deter other potential offers, thereby preserving the competitive nature of the bidding process.

In the 2023 ABA M&A Deal Points Study, only 20 percent of the deals analyzed included some form of termination fees, of which 14 percent were payable by both buyer and seller, while 73 percent was payable by the buyer only in certain events where the deal does not close. Consistent with the previously mentioned litigation cases, the amount of termination fees as a percentage of the deal value was a median of around 3 percent for the seller but a higher median of about 4 percent for the buyer for deals over $100 million.

Third-Party Consents

The consummation of the transaction may be conditioned on the receipt of stockholder approvals and/or third-party consents to the transaction. Recall that in Chapter 4 I advised you to review the material contracts in your agreement to understand the terms therein that may be triggered in an M&A. That self-diligence exercise should now pay good dividends at closing. The seller typically will be required by covenant to obtain all necessary consents from third parties with whom it has a contractual relationship. Here, it is extremely important for you to appreciate that this covenant could allow a third party to completely hold up the deal if their consent is required as a closing condition! In my experience, third parties do not intentionally hold up the deal, but very often they are unreachable or unable to respond promptly during the heat of closing and thereby unintentionally hold up the deal. As a seller, always ensure such a covenant has a reasonableness qualifier so you can close the deal after you make reasonable effort to obtain the third-party consent (even if you did not obtain it).

STOCKHOLDER APPROVAL

In a change of control event like an M&A, the target or constituent company is required to obtain the approval of its stockholders before it can consummate the transaction at closing. Such stockholder approval is a closing condition and the subject of a corresponding preclosing covenant. The minimum necessary approvals required from stockholders to consummate the transaction depends on (1) the structure of the M&A transaction (whether it's a merger, a private stock sale or an asset sale); (2) the applicable corporate statutes based on the target company's jurisdiction of formation and activity; and (3) the terms in the organizational documents, like certificate of incorporation and bylaws and any stockholder agreements. I discuss the key concepts for stockholder approval requirements here with an attempt to highlight best practices for stockholder approval solicitation in an M&A.

Stockholder Vote Requirements

The statutory voting requirements under state law varies from state to state.

Delaware has the most common, basic rule, where at least the majority of all shares voting together as one class must approve the transaction.

So, if we have a target corporation with 1,000 shares of

common stock, 200 shares of Series A preferred stock, and 100 shares of Series B preferred stock, then under the DGCL (with all other applicable terms not applying), the preferred stock would convert to common stock according to its conversion rights: assuming a 1:1 ratio, then all the common and preferred stock would vote together as a single class, so we have a base of 1,300 total voting shares, of which we need at least a majority, so at least 650 shares, to approve the transaction. Contrast this with California state law, where at least a majority of each class of stock must approve the transaction. So, in this example, if California law applies, we would need at least 500 shares of common stock, 100 shares of Series A preferred stock, and 50 shares of Series B preferred stock to approve the transaction.

In practice, the applicable state law contributes a great deal to how difficult it might be to get stockholder approval for the transaction. Under Delaware law, the target company could obtain the necessary 650 votes from a single common stockholder, like a founder, or any combination of large common and preferred stockholders across different classes or stock. However, under California law, even if all common stockholders voted to approve the deal with 1,000 votes, the target company would still not have sufficient votes to close the transaction because at least a majority of the Series A preferred stockholders or the Series B stockholders are not on board. This is one of the key practical considerations that motivate M&A lawyers to advise companies to convert to a Delaware corporation if they are out of state and considering an M&A.

These same minimum voting requirements can apply to an asset sale if that sale qualifies as a "de facto merger" under the two-part quantitate and qualitative test we introduced in Chapter 1 and applied in Chapter 6. Generally, a private stock sale resulting in a change of control by itself does not, under corporate statutes, require the approval of the target company's stockholders for any corporate action because the stockholders are making their individual decisions to sell their stock and directly entering into the stock purchase agreement or joinders. There may, however, be restrictions in the target company's certificate of incorporation that imposes some approval requirements for a change of control triggered by a private stock sale, especially if less than 100 percent is sold.

Once the minimum votes required under statute is determined, the target company has to layer on any additional voting requirements provided in its organizational documents in an M&A. We already discussed these additional voting requirements in a company's certificate of incorporation, called protective provisions, in Chapter 4 – as part of the preparation to sell your company. The protective provisions may require that, in our example, an M&A cannot be closed without the written approval of a specified Series A stockholder regardless of how many other votes approve the M&A; or it could increase the threshold to state that a supermajority or 75 percent of all the classes of stock voting together, not just a majority, must vote to approve the M&A. Such protective provisions are often negotiated during a venture equity financing or other investor financing event in a company and not in the event of an M&A.

Process Requirements

Once the votes required under statute and organizational documents is determined and applicable appraisal rights identified, the target company has to solicit the votes from its stockholders. In practice, the board of directors will first review and, if they so decide, approve the terms of the M&A

as set forth in the definitive acquisition agreement. Then, a key executive authorized by the board, most often the CEO, will sign and enter into the agreement on behalf of the target company, binding the target to the terms of the merger. Often, the major stockholders who are represented on the board will provide their stockholder consent immediately after because they already know all the terms of this deal they negotiated. Then, after this approval by the board and the major stockholders represented on the board, the target company will launch a "stockholder solicitation" to solicit votes to approve the deal from all other stockholders.

Stockholder Solicitation

This stockholder solicitation is an involved affair because most of these stockholders have only very recently heard about the M&A deal or not at all until they receive this communication from the target company. As a result, the target company, along with its M&A lawyer with feedback from the buyer's lawyer, will prepare a stockholder solicitation packet to inform the stockholder of the deal terms and their rights in connection to it so they can provide an informed vote. This packet often contains a statement summarizing all the material terms of the M&A deal in regular English (not legalese), a copy of the signed merger agreement and any other material exhibits or ancillary agreements – like a founder's executive compensation agreement with the buyer or an indemnification escrow agreement, an accounting of all applicable board and stockholder vote requirements and what the vote count is at the time of solicitation, a request from the target company to provide approval for the deal and an explanation of how to provide this approval.

Some state statutes also lay out the manner in which a

target company has to solicit stockholder approval for an M&A. The corporate statutes usually provide for a minimum ten-day's notice and maximum sixty-day's notice to hold a stockholder meeting to vote on the merger; these periods may be altered, though usually not shortened, in the certificate of incorporation or bylaws of a corporation. Under Delaware law, if electronic communication with stockholders is properly authorized, the target company can send this stockholder solicitation packet to stockholders by email and received votes by email or another electronic signature platform. If electronic communication is not authorized, then this becomes as much a logistical challenge as it is a legal one. A failure to observe a statutory notice period or process requirement may prevent the merger from being affected with the applicable secretary of state because often the certificate or agreement of merger requires a representation that the stockholder approval was obtained in a manner compliant with the corporate statute. Following the correct procedure is critical.

Appraisal Rights

Appraisal rights under Delaware corporate statutes, also known as dissenters' rights under the California corporate statutes, give a stockholder the right to be paid a "fair value" amount in cash that might differ from the consideration paid to the stockholder in an M&A.

In an asset sale that is a "de facto merger," the minimum voting requirements apply under Delaware law but in most cases appraisal rights do not apply. However, for such de facto merger both the minimum voting requirements and dissenter's rights apply under California law.

If appraisal rights apply in an M&A, then disclosure regarding the right to seek appraisal must be included in the stockholder solicitation packet so that a stockholder can perfect their appraisal rights if they do not approve the deal. The stockholder must adhere to strict technical processes to bring a claim of appraisal rights against the target company. Often, such claims end up in litigation because the claim centers on the difficult question of what the fair value of the shares ought to be at the time of closing. Because determination of such value is a factual rather than a legal matter, it is difficult to dispense with an appraisal rights case on the pleadings or in summary judgment, so it ends up going to trial.

If a stockholder is successful in its appraisal claim in a litigation, the target company has to pay additional cash to make up the difference between the consideration the stockholder received in the M&A for its shares and the higher fair value of such shares determined by trial.

The cash requirement is higher if the consideration was all or part stock. Stockholder appraisal rights claims and any attendant costs or losses in litigation of such claims are most often subject to indemnification in a merger agreement, so the target company (or seller) has to suffer them and not the buyer.

The good news is that appraisal rights can be waived by stockholders. The best practice is to require all stockholders to waive their appraisal rights at the same time that they provide their approval for the transaction through the stockholder solicitation process. However, even if a stockholder does not waive their appraisal rights when solicited, you can work in the waiver of such appraisal rights in an M&A in an existing or upcoming stockholder agreement. This is because Delaware law leans very heavily in favor of preserving negotiated contractual waivers when it comes to appraisal rights – though they are considered a fundamental right for stockholders. Due to a rise in "appraisal arbitrage," where mutual funds and private hedge funds bought stock in pending acquisitions of target companies solely to exercise appraisal rights, the Delaware courts have become more skeptical of appraisal claims asserted by sophisticated parties who are skilled at putting forth alternative valuation theories in an attempt to prove that the merger price was undervalued. The Delaware courts have recently found that the merger price agreed upon after a robust *Revlon* process is "highly probative" of the fair value of the company. I will discuss such *Revlon* duties, at long last, in the next chapter.

It should also be noted that in certain transactions that are challenged by a stockholder as breach of the fiduciary duties by the board of directors in approving such transactions, obtaining appropriate stockholder approval can play a very effective role in determining that the board did not breach their fiduciary duties in approving that transaction. I will go into more details about a board's fiduciary duties and best practices to avoid breach of such duties in the next chapter.

280G

One issue that frequently catches founders off guard in an M&A is the possibility that their hard-earned and hard-won proceeds and earnings in an M&A will have to be publicly disclosed to all the stockholders in his target company.

Like most people, founders prefer not to tell anyone, especially current or past employees who remain as minority stockholders on the company's cap table, about how much they are making. However, in deals where the target sells for many multiples of its company valuation, there are certain requirements under Section 280G of the Internal Revenue Code that could compel you to disclose the purchase price proceeds you receive as an officer and stockholder along with your future executive compensation package. Section 280G is a weird aspect of US law where a federal tax statute ends up governing corporate action during an M&A. You will recall that in Chapter 3 we discussed how state law governs corporate actions; 280G is an exception to this rule.

Section 280G addresses the tax implications of "parachute payments" made to certain individuals in the event of a change in control of a corporation. Specifically, it targets payments that are contingent on a change in ownership or control and exceed a certain threshold, which is typically three times the individual's base amount, defined as the average annual compensation over the previous five years.

In the context of a private company M&A, Section 280G can have significant implications. If a payment qualifies as an "excess parachute payment," the recipient is subject to a 20 percent excise tax on the amount that exceeds their base amount, and the corporation cannot deduct this excess amount for tax purposes.

Section 280G of the Internal Revenue Code addresses "golden parachute payments," which are substantial payments made to key employees, typically executives, in the event of an M&A. The purpose of Section 280G is to discourage excessive compensation that might detract from shareholder value and align executive incentives more closely with stockholder interests. This can create substantial tax liabilities for both the individual and the corporation involved in the transaction.

A "disqualified individual" under Section 280G includes officers, stockholders, and highly compensated employees of the corporation. A founder is often a disqualified individual. The statute is designed to prevent these individuals from receiving disproportionately large payments that could be seen as a reward for the change in control rather than for services rendered. The regulations also allow for certain payments to be excluded from the definition of parachute payments if they can be shown to be reasonable compensation for services performed after the change in control.

One notable aspect of Section 280G is the stockholder approval exception, which is particularly relevant for private companies. If more than 75 percent of the disinterested stockholders approve the parachute payments, the payments may be exempt from the adverse tax consequences of Section 280G. Essentially, the requisite vote – 75 percent – of the disinterested stockholders in the M&A transaction can "cleanse" golden parachute payments during an M&A of its adverse tax consequences. This provision allows private companies some flexibility in structuring their M&A transactions to avoid the punitive excise tax and loss of deductions.

This cleansing vote solicitation is tricky to execute. On my first M&A deal as a newbie associate, I had to prepare and mail out more than three hundred disclosure statements to shareholders of the California company being sold. They were being mailed to various countries across the world at the same time. I had to make sure that all three-hundred-plus disclosure packets, containing over five hundred pages of legal documents, each were identical and complete and there were no errors or omissions. Even a single missed mailing to a stockholder would require me to do the entire mailing all over again due to the strict 280G procedural rules. I was so stressed after I completed the mailing, that night I had a nightmare about it and drove to the office at 4:00 a.m. in the morning to make sure that the missed disclosure packet from my nightmare wasn't lurking around in my office or the mailroom. This is exemplary of the level of stress that general corporate lawyers who do not specialize in M&A can face in situations like a 280G mailing. However, after doing M&A for the better part of a decade now, I have seen most of the common pitfalls that could lead a company to redo the 280G vote solicitation.

However, in practice, companies often take steps to mitigate the impact of Section 280G. For example, they may structure payments to fall below the threshold that triggers the excise tax or seek disinterested stockholder approval to qualify for the exemption. Additionally, companies may provide detailed calculations and disclosures to ensure compliance with the regulations and to support the reasonableness of the compensation paid to disqualified individuals.

All the founders I have advised have truly disliked this cleansing vote in practice and it's no surprise why. If your employees learn about all the money you stand to make from the sale of the company through the 280G disclosure and are dissatisfied with what they stand to make, it will be an uncomfortable and challenging experience for you to lead that team through successfully closing an M&A. However, in most cases, founders are able to rally their troops and obtain the requisite cleansing vote, often after much hand wringing.

Since the surviving corporation will be in the buyer's control, a buyer is particularly concerned about compliance to 280G if it applies to an M&A. This results in 280G becoming a preclosing covenant where seller promises to undertake a "cleansing vote" by its stockholders and the requisite approval of the stockholder of the golden parachute payments made to each individual a closing condition to the M&A.

THE LAST NUGGET

I hope you found our discussion of preclosing covenants and closing conditions in this chapter helpful in imagining what the last stretch of an M&A deal might be like. In this chapter I presented and discussed a few high impact preclosing covenants that you might be subject to as a seller in an M&A, like a 280G stockholder cleansing vote solicitation. Closing an M&A deal is not easy. Both buyer and seller, and their many different advisors, focus on various different slices of the transaction, and have to find their way to a mutually agreeable plane. Achieving that agreement in something that is as complicated as the sale of an entire company or business is no mean feat. I sometimes analogize a deal closing to the steeple-chase track and field event in the Olympics. You can feel like you have run 7.5 laps around a standard four-hundred-meter track and cleared twenty-eight fixed barriers and seven water jumps to get to the closing. Once you have crossed the finish line, you are able to enjoy the proceeds of the M&A.

12

FIDUCIARY DUTIES OF DIRECTORS IN A M&A

The corporate laws that govern a director's or officer's conduct during an M&A depend on the capitalization of the target company, the transaction's structure, and the deal's material terms.

I hope my prior warning in Chapter 3 on this chapter being filled with litigation case law doesn't turn you off. You may safely read this chapter with at least some mild curiosity and interest.

You don't have to remember all of this. This is because

your M&A lawyer should advise you and your board of directors on your respective fiduciary duties in an M&A.

Even though it can raise the legal bill, I advise you to ask your M&A lawyer to make this presentation to your board, ideally before you sign an LOI. Depending on the complexity of your transaction, it can be a short email memo or a live presentation with slides followed by a Q&A.

I also advise you to ask your M&A lawyer to make another presentation to your board of directors on the final proposed material terms of the M&A under consideration before signing the definitive agreement. This one should be a live presentation with slides followed by a Q&A. In that Q&A, you should absolutely ask any questions you have about your fiduciary duties under applicable law and encourage your board of directors to do the same. Then, the board of directors deliberate and vote on the transaction in accordance with their fiduciary duties. For most small or lower-middle-market private company sale transactions, this is the advised minimum.

Depending on the facts, a more or less deliberate legal advising process may be required or advisable. For some of my smallest clients with solo or two-person boards, like a husband and wife, this is not as critical because they have already been deeply involved in the negotiation of the M&A. However, for a board of directors representing differing stockholder interests, it is important to lower the probability of a litigation brought by a stockholder alleging that the board breached its fiduciary duties toward them.

In the context of M&A involving private Delaware corporations, the fiduciary duties of the board of directors, executives, and controlling stockholders are of paramount importance. These duties are primarily centered on the duties of care, loyalty, candor, and good faith. This chapter outlines these fiduciary duties as they apply to M&A transactions under Delaware law. Here, I focus on the fundamentals only. In many other states, the general two duties of care and loyalty apply without any added substantive or procedural requirements.

I focus primarily on these fiduciary duties – the duties of care, loyalty, candor and good faith – and the infamous *Revlon* duty – during the sale of a target company to an unrelated buyer and then discuss the particular fiduciary duties in the sale of the controlling stockholder's interest in the target company to an unrelated party where the duties are usually more narrowly focused on being fiduciaries to the minority stockholders.

In an M&A, the board has various means of establishing that the board fulfilled these duties toward its stockholders.

The general standard applied in order to determine whether a board fulfilled its duties is the "business judgment rule."

Because of potential board conflicts in an M&A (e.g., directors may lose their positions after the M&A when the buyer votes for its own directors, and the officer-directors, such as a founder, may, after the closing, lose their highly compensated positions as officers of the company or gain even more compensation as employees of the buyer),

Delaware has instituted certain substantive and procedural requirements called "enhanced scrutiny" before the board will be given business judgment rule protection for its decisions in an M&A.

DUTY OF CARE

The board has a duty of care to act on an informed manner, with the care a reasonably

prudent person would use under similar circumstances.

Directors must fully inform themselves of all material information reasonably available before making a decision. In the M&A context, this includes conducting thorough due diligence and considering all relevant factors to ensure that the transaction is in the best interests of the corporation and its stockholders.

In determining whether a target board has been informed in making its decisions – the seminal guidance is provided from the Delaware case of *Smith v. Van Gorkom* (Delaware 1985). TransUnion Corporation, a publicly held company, approved a merger proposal where its shareholders would receive $55 per share in cash. The proposal was presented by the company's CEO, Mr. Jerome Van Gorkom, who had personally negotiated the terms of the merger with the buyer without prior authorization from the company's board of directors. Then, when he proposed the deal, the board approved the merger after a two-hour meeting without prior notice of the meeting's purpose or time to review the merger agreement. The CEO's presentation was based on his own understanding of the merger agreement, which he had not thoroughly reviewed, and the board relied on his brief explanation without seeking further information. Mr. Smith and a handful of other stockholders of Trans Union Corporation brought a class action against the directors of Trans Union, alleging that the board breached their fiduciary duties by failing to make an informed decision in approving the merger.

The Delaware Supreme Court held that the board's decision to approve the merger was not the product of an informed business judgment. The target company's board failed to evaluate whether the $55 per share was a fair price for the stockholders given that the number had been initially settled on by Mr. Van Gorkom as a price at which he would sell his stock. The directors acted in a grossly negligent manner by approving the merger with minimal review and without adequate information. The court emphasized that directors have a duty to act in an informed and deliberate manner, especially in decisions involving mergers. The court also held that the directors failed to disclose all material facts to the stockholders before seeking their approval for the merger, further contributing to the breach of fiduciary duties.

DUTY OF LOYALTY

The duty of loyalty mandates that directors act in the best interests of the corporation and its stockholders, avoiding any conflicts of interest.

Directors must not use their position to further personal interests at the expense of the corporation. In M&A transactions, this duty is particularly critical when directors have personal interests in the transaction. Directors must ensure that any self-interested transactions are entirely fair to the corporation and its minority stockholders.

A director of a target company will often be in a position of conflict if:

- The director owns preferred stock in the target company and seeks to approve a merger in which the preferred stock will receive a significant premium over the common stock.
- The director is also an officer of the target company whose job and salary are at risk of being

lost or potentially enhanced after consummation
of a merger.
- The director will receive a finder's fee or other
type of compensation upon the consummation of
a merger.

To address conflicts, an independent (i.e., nonconflicted) committee of the board is often chartered by the full board to negotiate and approve the M&A transaction. If the entire board is unconflicted, then there is no need for an independent committee.

Duty of Candor

Recall that in Chapter 11 we discussed the preclosing covenant and closing condition requiring the solicitation of stockholder approval for the M&A as a preclosing covenant and the receipt of the requisite stockholder approval as a closing condition. After the board approves a deal and authorizes the CEO to enter into a definitive agreement, if stockholder approval is required to close, then the directors have a fiduciary duty to disclose fully and fairly all material information within their control when seeking stockholder action.

This duty is heightened in the context of M&A transactions, where stockholders must make informed decisions about whether to approve the transaction or seek appraisal rights. The information disclosed must be sufficient to allow stockholders to understand the value of their shares and the implications of the transaction.

Duty of Good Faith

In addition to being informed, board members must also

act in good faith, which means that the board members cannot consciously disregard or act recklessly with regard to their duties of care and loyalty. In other words,

> **board members must not only be informed but must take actions to be informed and to deliberate with the other board members and act in a manner intended to benefit the company when causing the sale of the company.**

A breach of the duty of good faith can take many forms. Three primary examples of a breach of the duty of good faith are:

- Action taken by a director with a purpose other than that of advancing the best interests of the corporation.
- A director's intentional violation of applicable positive law.
- Failure by a director to act in the face of a known duty to act, in conscious disregard for such director's duties.

THE *REVLON* DUTY IN AN M&A

> **In addition to the two duties of care and loyalty to stockholders, in the event of an M&A Delaware imposes another duty on the board of the target company: a duty to seek the best terms in the deal.**

The best terms are not just the highest price but also additional considerations like the likelihood of closing the deal (which can be affected by preclosing covenants like getting required third party consents), whether the deal is fully financed (which can be the cash-stock consideration mix or the buyer's need to obtain financing), and whether the deal has material contingencies (such as a closing condition that requires anti-trust approval for the deal).

This additional duty is known as the *Revlon* duty, which we referenced a few times throughout the book where applicable. The original *Revlon* court decision had held that the board had to act as auctioneers in a selling process – selling the target company to the highest bidder. However, this *Revlon* doctrine has since been modified by later court decisions to move away from a prescriptive process to a duty to seek the best terms reasonably available to the board.

The case centers on the takeover battle for Revlon Inc., a Delaware corporation. The primary conflict was between Pantry Pride Inc., led by Ronald O. Perelman, and Forstmann Little & Co., a private equity firm. Initially, Pantry Pride attempted to acquire Revlon through a friendly acquisition, but Revlon's CEO, Michel C. Bergerac, dismissed the offer as too low. Subsequently, Pantry Pride made a hostile tender offer, which prompted Revlon to adopt several defensive measures, including a stock repurchase plan and a "poison pill" rights plan, designed to make the takeover more difficult. (I don't talk about these in this book because they are most relevant for public companies.)

As the bidding war intensified, Revlon began negotiations with Forstmann Little & Co., ultimately agreeing to a leveraged buyout that included a higher price per share for Revlon stockholders. This agreement also included a lock-up option, a no-shop provision, and a $25 million cancellation fee, effectively ending the auction for Revlon. MacAndrews & Forbes Holdings Inc., the parent company of Pantry Pride, filed a lawsuit seeking to enjoin these defensive measures, arguing that they breached the fiduciary duties of Revlon's board by prioritizing the interests of other constituencies, like noteholders, over the interests of the stockholders.

The Court of Chancery of Delaware granted the injunction, preventing Revlon from completing the transaction with Forstmann. The defendants appealed the decision to the Delaware Supreme Court. The Delaware Supreme Court affirmed the decision of the Court of Chancery, holding that Revlon's board of directors breached their fiduciary duties by favoring Forstmann over Pantry Pride, thus failing to maximize shareholder value during the auction process.

The court emphasized that directors have fiduciary duties of care and loyalty to the corporation and its stockholders. These duties are particularly critical during a corporate control transaction, where the board's role shifts from protecting the corporate entity to maximizing shareholder value. The court found that while lock-ups and related agreements are permissible under Delaware law, they must be untainted by director interest and should not breach fiduciary duties. In this case, the lock-up agreement with Forstmann ended the bidding process prematurely, which was not in the stockholders' best interest. The court acknowledged that considering the impact of a takeover on other constituencies, such as employees or creditors, is permissible, but only if it benefits stockholders. In *Revlon*, these considerations did not benefit the stockholders and were thus deemed improper. When the sale of a company becomes inevitable, the board's duty is to act as auctioneers to obtain the highest possible price for stockholders. Revlon's board failed in this duty by agreeing to terms with Forstmann that were not open to competitive bidding and thus not in the best interest of the stockholders.

The Delaware Supreme Court's decision in *Revlon* established a precedent that during a takeover, once the decision to sell has been made, the directors' primary obligation is to maximize the value for the stockholders, and they cannot favor one bidder over another without a clear and compelling reason that benefits the stockholders. The defensive measures taken by Revlon's board were therefore struck down as inconsistent with their fiduciary duties. However, as I mentioned earlier, this duty to get the best price evolved to become the duty to get the best terms.

Fifteen years later in 2010, stockholders of Dollar Thrifty Automotive Group Inc. filed a class action against the target company's board of directors over a proposed merger with Hertz Global Holdings Inc. The merger offered Dollar Thrifty stockholders $32.80 per share in cash and 0.6366 shares of Hertz stock, totaling $41 per share. Stockholders claimed the board failed to maximize stockholder value by not conducting a presigning auction and accepting a modest premium. A competing bid from Avis Budget Group Inc. offered $46.50 per share, but Avis did not provide sufficient assurances regarding antitrust approval, unlike Hertz. The court denied the stockholders' request for a preliminary injunction, finding that the Dollar Thrifty board acted reasonably and with proper consideration in favoring Hertz's bid.

The board evaluated potential risks and benefits, concluding that Hertz's offer provided greater deal certainty, which was crucial given the antitrust risks associated with Avis. The court found the termination fee and matching rights did not deter serious bidders, as evidenced by Avis's competing offer. The board's actions were consistent with their duty to maximize stockholder value. They prioritized certainty of closing, which justified accepting a slightly lower bid from Hertz. Unlike in *Revlon*, where the board prematurely ended the bidding process, the Dollar Thrifty board was found to have acted reasonably by prioritizing deal certainty over a potentially higher bid with greater risks. The court upheld the board's decision to include deal protection measures, contrasting with *Revlon*, where such measures were deemed to improperly favor one bidder.

In a situation where a controlling stockholder is selling its shares to a third-party, or in the purchase by a controlling stockholder of the minority interests in the corporations, there is no "sale of control" for which the board of the target has influence, and thus the board is deemed to be the fiduciary to the minority shareholders in these situations. The Delaware courts have held in these situations the *Revlon* duties do not apply to the target board that has no ability to "shop" the company or seek better terms because the controlling stockholder controls the transaction.

STANDARDS OF JUDICIAL REVIEW

In 1983, two years before the *Revlon* decision, the Delaware Supreme Court introduced the "entire fairness" standard in *Weinberger v. UOP*. This case involved a cash-out merger between UOP Inc. and its majority stockholder, Signal Companies Inc., which owned 50.5 percent of UOP. Signal sought to acquire the remaining minority shares for twenty-one dollars per share. Minority stockholders, led by William B. Weinberger, challenged the merger, arguing the price was unfair and that UOP's board failed to disclose a feasibility study suggesting Signal could pay up to twenty-four dollars per share. The Delaware Supreme Court reversed the lower court's decision, holding that the merger did not meet the "entire fairness" standard due to conflicts of interest and lack of full disclosure. The court emphasized that directors on both sides of a transaction must demonstrate fairness in both process and price, and failure to disclose the study breached their duty to minority shareholders.

Two years later, in *Revlon*, the court clarified that enhanced scrutiny applies when a board must secure the best price in an inevitable sale. This principle expanded in *In re Dollar Thrifty* (a case we presented in the previous chapter), where enhanced scrutiny was extended to cover all deal terms, including price. In *Corwin v. KKR*, the Delaware Supreme Court ruled that an informed, uncoerced vote of disinterested stockholders could "cleanse" a board's decision, even if conflicts of interest exist in an M&A.

In *Corwin*, KKR Financial Holdings LLC stockholders argued the board breached its fiduciary duties by approving a merger with KKR & Co. L.P. The Delaware Court of Chancery dismissed the case, applying the business judgment rule after disinterested stockholders approved the merger. The Delaware Supreme Court upheld the ruling, noting that KKR was not a controlling stockholder and that the disinterested stockholder vote triggered the business judgment rule, eliminating the need for enhanced scrutiny.

FIDUCIARY DUTIES OF CONTROLLING STOCKHOLDERS

Often in small private company M&A, there are controlling stockholders who can influence the governance of the corporation. In Delaware, controlling stockholders owe fiduciary duties to both the corporation and its minority stockholders. These duties primarily include the duty of loyalty and the duty of care that I have laid out here. When a controlling stockholder stands on both sides of a transaction with the corporation, such as in mergers or other significant corporate actions, the transaction must meet the "entire fairness" standard of judicial.

The *In re Martha Stewart Living Omnimedia, Inc. Stockholder Litigation* case (2017) addresses fiduciary duties of controlling stockholders in the context of M&A, specifically the obligations they have to minority shareholders during a sale process. The case centers on Martha Stewart, the controlling stockholder of Martha Stewart Living Omnimedia (MSLO), during its acquisition by Sequential Brands Group Inc.

Stockholders alleged that Stewart breached her fiduciary duties by negotiating personal side deals with Sequential, including post-merger employment agreements, that benefited her disproportionately compared to the minority shareholders. The plaintiffs claimed Stewart leveraged her controlling position to secure these arrangements while accepting a lower price for MSLO shares than initially offered.

The court, however, ruled in Stewart's favor, applying the *Kahn v. M&F Worldwide Corp.* "business judgment rule." This rule applies when certain procedural safeguards, such as the formation of an independent special committee and the requirement of approval by a majority of the minority shareholders, are in place from the beginning of negotiations. In this case, the court found that these protections had been followed precisely, ensuring that the transaction was fair to minority shareholders and that Stewart did not receive any inappropriate consideration.

The key takeaway for founders is the importance of structuring transactions with safeguards like independent special committees and minority stockholder approval to avoid potential breaches of fiduciary duty claims. Controlling stock-holders must act fairly, ensuring that personal benefits do not outweigh the interests of other shareholders.

The *In re Tesla Motors, Inc. Stockholder Litigation* (2022) case highlights fiduciary duties of controlling stockholders in the context of M&A, centering on Tesla's acquisition of Solar-City, a solar energy company. Tesla's shareholders sued Elon Musk, claiming he breached his fiduciary duty as a controlling stockholder by pushing Tesla to acquire SolarCity, a company founded by Musk and other family members, which was facing liquidity issues at the time.

Plaintiffs alleged that Musk used his influence to force the Tesla board into an unfair transaction that was designed to bail out SolarCity and protect his personal investment. Although Musk only owned approximately 22 percent of Tesla's stock, the court found that his level of control and influence over Tesla's board could classify him as a controlling stockholder. This finding triggered the "entire fairness" stan-dard of review, which required Musk to prove that the trans-action was fair in both process and price.

Despite finding procedural flaws, such as Musk's deep involvement in negotiations and conflicts of interest within Tesla's board, the court ultimately ruled that the acquisition was entirely fair. The court emphasized that the price Tesla paid for SolarCity was fair, and the transaction aligned with Tesla's long-term goal of becoming a vertically integrated sustainable energy company.

This case underscores the importance of maintaining fair-ness in M&A transactions when a controlling stockholder is involved. It also demonstrates that minority shareholders can challenge transactions where conflicts of interest may lead to breaches of fiduciary duty, but a fair price can ultimately vali-date the deal. Founders and leaders involved in M&A must be mindful of conflicts and ensure proper procedural safeguards, such as independent committees and disinterested stockholder votes, to avoid fiduciary duty violations.

More recently in *Crispo v. Musk*, the Delaware Court of Chancery examined fiduciary duties in M&A transactions, specifically focusing on whether Elon Musk, in his attempted acquisition of Twitter, breached fiduciary duties as a controlling stockholder. This case highlights critical issues for founders and directors when navigating fiduciary obligations in the context of M&A.

In April 2022, Elon Musk, through X Holdings I Inc. and X Holdings II Inc., agreed to acquire Twitter. However, in July 2022, Musk attempted to terminate the merger, prompting a lawsuit from Luigi Crispo, a Twitter stockholder. Crispo claimed Musk breached fiduciary duties as a controlling stockholder and sought specific performance of the merger agreement.

Crispo argued that Musk, as a controlling stockholder, violated his fiduciary duties by attempting to back out of the Twitter acquisition. Under Delaware law, a controlling stockholder has heightened fiduciary obligations to act in the best interests of minority stockholders during transactions like mergers. Crispo contended that Musk, due to his substantial influence over Twitter and the deal, should be considered a controlling stockholder and, therefore, owed fiduciary duties to Twitter's minority stockholders.

The court ultimately dismissed the fiduciary duty claim, concluding that Crispo failed to establish Musk's status as a controlling stockholder. Despite Musk's significant influence, the court found that he did not exercise sufficient control over Twitter's day-to-day operations or decision-making processes prior to the merger. As such, Musk did not have the fiduciary obligations typically imposed on controlling stockholders. The

Crispo v. Musk case has not seen a higher court review beyond the Delaware Court of Chancery at the time of writing.

UNSOLICITED BIDS

Remember my imaginary yet typical client Sarah and her start-up that designs and manufactures prosthetics for children from Chapter 1? What is Sarah's duty as a director on the board, an executive, and a stockholder of her target company when she receives an unsolicited bid?

In the context of an unsolicited bid to buy a target company, the founder who is a director, executive, and stockholder has specific fiduciary duties under Delaware law. These duties primarily include the duties of care and loyalty, which are heightened in the context of a sale of control.

The duty of care requires directors to act with the care that a reasonably prudent person would use in similar circumstances. This includes being fully informed and making decisions based on adequate information. In the context of an unsolicited bid, the founder must thoroughly evaluate the offer, seek expert advice if necessary, and ensure that the decision-making process is well-documented.

The duty of loyalty mandates that directors act in the best interests of the corporation and its shareholders, avoiding conflicts of interest. When a founder is involved in a potential sale, they must ensure that their personal interests do not conflict with those of the shareholders. If there is a potential conflict, such as negotiating post-merger employment, the founder must disclose this and possibly recuse themselves from certain decisions to ensure impartiality.

Under the *Revlon* standard, when a company is up for sale, the directors' primary duty is to secure the best value reasonably available for the shareholders. This involves a thorough and unbiased evaluation of the bid and potentially seeking alternative offers to ensure the highest value is achieved. The courts will apply enhanced scrutiny to ensure that the directors have acted reasonably and in good faith to achieve this goal.

However, if Sarah is also a controlling stockholder, then she has an additional duty to safeguard the interests of minority stockholders. If Sarah herself receives an employment offer to join the potential buyer to continue with the surviving company after the M&A, she has a conflict of interest in the M&A and the entire fairness standard of fair price and fair process will likely apply instead of the business judgment rule. The board has no standing obligation to entertain bids, even generous ones, but must fulfil their fiduciary duties in decision-making.

In summary, Sarah as the founder must act with due care, remain loyal to the shareholders' interests, and strive to secure the best possible value in the sale. This includes being transparent about any conflicts of interest and ensuring that the decision-making process is thorough and well-documented to withstand judicial scrutiny.

BEST PRACTICES

To fulfill its fiduciary duties and thereby ensure the protection of the business judgment rule or a favorable ruling in the event that a heightened level of entire fairness standard scrutiny applies, a selling company's board of directors should:

- **Take adequate time** to consider and review all available information relevant to the merger;

- **Determine the need to rely on any outside advisors** or internal or external experts and engage such advisors or experts to enhance the board's decision-making ability where appropriate;
- **Consider any conflicts** or other factors that could influence the advice of their advisors and experts, both internal and external (it may be advisable to exclude conflicted directors from the decision-making process at the earliest possible date in order to fully comply with its duty of loyalty);
- **Actively engage** in all presentations (including those given by internal and external advisors), asking questions and seeking clarification or additional information when needed;
- **Document the board's process** in minutes that detail their process, considerations and deliberations; and
- **Review drafts** of all principal transaction documents and explanations of intricate or complicated provisions.

In addition to these general guidelines, other steps should be taken when special circumstances arise. For example, where heightened judicial review may apply, the target company's board should have a record of its knowledge and understanding of the target company's value, including, if applicable, through advice and valuations performed by outside financial advisors. It should show a process of having engaged with potential transaction parties, either through extensive one-on-one discussions or as part of an organized auction process. It should show an understanding of the transaction arrangements and alternatives available to it so that it can show that it made informed decisions about the relative costs and benefits of any preclusive or coercive transactions terms, such as exclusivity and no shop provisions, break-up fees, and voting agreements. Your M&A lawyer should suggest guidelines appropriate for your target company and transaction.

13

ACHIEVING YOUR DREAMS WITH M&A

As you reach the final chapter of this book, let's reflect on the journey we've taken together. Each chapter of this book has been carefully crafted to equip you with the knowledge, tools, and confidence to navigate the complex realm of mergers and acquisitions (M&A). The path to selling your start-up is challenging, but as you've learned, it is also filled with opportunities for growth, learning, and, ultimately, success.

The first three chapters of this set the stage for you to understand the realm in which this book operates. In the first chapter, you were introduced to the dynamic world of M&A, especially in the context of private companies in the technology sector. The chapter set the stage by highlighting the economic fluctuations and market conditions that can impact M&A activity. You were also introduced to the essential players in the M&A process, and I emphasized the importance of understanding these fundamentals before diving into the details of your transaction. The value you gained here is a foundational understanding of the M&A landscape, which is crucial for making informed decisions throughout your journey.

Chapter 2 was a personal introduction, offering insight into my background and the experiences that have shaped my approach to M&A. By sharing my story – from my roots in Bangladesh to practicing law in Silicon Valley – I aimed to demonstrate that M&A is not just a technical field but also a deeply human one, where empathy and understanding of diverse perspectives are essential. This chapter provided you with the reassurance that your M&A journey is supported by someone who understands both the professional and personal stakes involved.

Chapter 3 laid out the roadmap for the M&A process, guiding you through the different stages of a transaction – from the Shopping Period to the Post-Closing Period. We explored the various types of M&A transactions – a merger, private stock sale, and asset sale – and the legal frameworks that govern them, particularly in Delaware and California. Understanding these stages and their significance was essential to prepare you for the journey ahead to understanding the key concepts that are highly valuable and have a significant impact on the success of an M&A transaction.

The next three chapters, Chapters 4, 5 and 6, walked you through the Shopping Period in an M&A. Preparation is the cornerstone of a successful M&A transaction. In Chapter 4, we delved into the concept of "self-diligence" – the process of scrutinizing your own company before potential buyers do. You learned about the importance of making your business as presentable and your business case for acquisition as robust as possible, from financial statements to legal documents. This chapter also covered the long-term preparation strategies that can position your company favorably for an M&A, such as negotiating liquidation preference during an equity financing, even if a sale is not immediately on the horizon.

Selecting the right buyer is crucial to achieving your goals in an M&A transaction. Chapter 5 focused on strategies for identifying buyers who align with your vision for the company's future, whether that's continuing its mission or maximizing financial returns. The chapter also discussed the importance of assembling a team of advisors, including an M&A lawyer and possibly an investment banker, to help navigate this critical decision-making process.

At the end of the Shopping Period, the letter of intent (LOI) is the first major milestone in the M&A process. In Chapter 6, we discussed the importance of the LOI, which, although often nonbinding other than for exclusivity and confidentiality obligations, sets the tone for the entire transaction. You learned about the key terms typically negotiated in an LOI, such as the top-line purchase price, transaction structure, and type of deal consideration, and how these can influence the final deal. This chapter emphasized the importance of approaching the LOI with intelligence, integrity, and strategic thinking.

The next two chapters, Chapters 7 and 8, are the real moneymakers for you. These two chapters contain the highest value content in this entire book. Chapter 7 was dedicated to understanding the various aspects of the purchase price – the top-line figure often cited in M&A announcements and the more nuanced "take-home" amount that sellers actually receive. We explored different forms of consideration, payment structures and how adjustments can significantly impact the final amount you walk away with. This chapter gave you the tools to better understand and negotiate the financial aspects of your deal by understanding how the company's valuation based on its financial statements connect to the purchase price, which is then adjusted to reflect a fair deal between the buyer and seller.

In addition to maximizing the dollar amount, risk management is the other critical aspect of any M&A transaction. Chapter 8 introduced the critical concept of risk-shifting in M&A transactions. It emphasized the role of indemnification provisions as a primary tool for managing and allocating risk between the buyer and seller. Indemnification clauses are designed to protect one party from losses or damages arising from breaches of representations, warranties, or covenants by the other party. Mastering indemnification provisions and understanding the role of fraud in M&A are essential for effectively managing and mitigating post-closing risks.

In Chapters 9, 10 and 11, the focus was on the common bases for a buyer to bring indemnification claims against a seller – breach of representations and warranties and breach of covenants. In Chapter 9, the focus is on representations and warranties and the attendant disclosure schedules. Representations and warranties are statements of fact made by one party to another, covering various aspects of the target company's business, finances, and operations. These statements are critical because any breach can trigger indemnification obligations. Understanding the intricacies of representations, warranties, and disclosure schedules is key to uncovering hidden risks and effectively managing indemnification obligations.

Chapter 10 discussed the role of covenants in M&A transactions, particularly those operating after the closing. Covenants are promises or commitments made by the parties, often relating to the conduct of the business during the Interim Period. This chapter covers different types of covenants, in particular the post-closing restrictive covenants like noncompete that can bind a key executive or seller.

Chapter 10 also discussed unique considerations for a key executive who is negotiating their post-closing employment and compensation terms with a buyer. In Chapter 11, the discussion continued with preclosing covenants with a focus on how to successfully close the transaction. The chapter provided practical guidance on satisfying closing conditions and managing any last-minute negotiations that might arise.

In the penultimate chapter, we turned our attention to the fiduciary duties of directors during an M&A transaction. Chapter 12 provided an overview of the legal obligations that directors owe to their target company and its stockholders, particularly in the context of Delaware law. Understanding these duties is essential for ensuring that the board's decisions are legally sound and in the best interests of the company, thereby minimizing the risk of litigation claiming a breach of fiduciary duties and maximizing the chances of a successful deal.

TIPS AND TRICKS MAY STRENGTHEN MY BONES, 'CAUSE WORDS ON PAPER CAN HURT ME

I will say farewell to you with a note on the five key tips and tricks that you can use as a founder of a start-up to successfully start and close an M&A. This is not the best five or the most recommended five items, but instead the five items I know, based on my experience, that can empower you to win at M&A.

Continue to Learn about M&A

Nothing beats knowledge empowerment when it comes to winning in the realm of mergers and acquisitions (M&A) – a realm created and governed by laws. By reading this book, you are already well on your way to navigating and winning at M&A like a seasoned entrepreneur. This knowledge, for most founders going through an M&A for the first time, is picked up on the job, where they are constantly reacting to complex decision points placed in front of them under time pressure. You are not going to be that founder. So far, you have received an overview of the M&A market and an understand of the journey from start to finish; you have understood some key concepts that have a high impact on the purchase price proceeds you get to take-home and that shift risk to you in a manner that can claw back the proceeds you receive even after the closing of an M&A; you have been given a cheat sheet of high impact negotiation strategies that help you maximize your company valuation and minimize your deal risk; and you have gotten an idea about the practical experience of what it could be like to going through an M&A as a seller or founder of a target company.

In the previous chapter, I give you a primer on the corporate rules that govern your role as a director in an M&A. You will be in control, not reactive. However, this is just the beginning of your learning about M&A. As I caution throughout, this book only provides an overview of issues I deem relevant; it is hardly a comprehensive or detailed guide. I encourage you to take heart from this book and continue to educate yourself on areas of M&A that can be helpful for your business.

Assess Periodically, Prepare Thoughtfully

Preparation is everything you have done that brings you to the closing of an M&A. Not all preparation will be helpful in closing an M&A, but each preparation will be helpful to your business. By its very nature, any steps you take to prepare for an M&A will contribute to making your start-up better.

Though a single chapter is titled "Preparing for Sale," this entire book prepares you in many ways for an M&A. I specifically point to self-diligence as an effective preparation tool in Chapter 4, which is titled "Preparing for Sale," but in reality, there are recommendations on how to prepare scattered throughout the book.

For example, I note in Chapter 10 how granting equity compensation awards to key executives in your start-up can affect the post-closing employment offers they receive at an M&A. How much you invest in preparation and when you prepare are determinations unique to your circumstances. You should consult with your advisors to come up with a preparation strategy that works for you. However, nothing beats preparation when opportunity comes knocking.

Assemble the Right Team and Communicate

M&A is a team sport. In addition to transaction specific advisers such as an investment banker, an M&A lawyer, specialists in transactional tax and executive compensation, an escrow agent, and a professional stockholder representative, you also have your existing business team members and advisors who can help you to plan for and execute on an M&A. Just like building a start-up, you need to curate the talent required to execute your vision of an M&A. You need to maintain effective communication between you and your team members – or delegate that to your M&A lawyer – to ensure that your advisory team understands your vision and is executing on it as you direct. In an M&A, where there is so much complex information and processes happening in parallel at break-neck speed, having the right team and solid communication and coordination between its members is absolutely essential to success.

Set Ambitious but Achievable Goals

One of the biggest traps a founder can set for themselves in an M&A is not determining what success could look like. Buyers don't make this mistake. They come into a deal knowing the business synergies they seek from a potential transaction. However, founders of start-ups are not provided this lesson, so they often enter into an M&A not really knowing what their business goals are beyond getting acquired for a glob of money. But as you now know, an M&A entails so much more than that. When that founder is asked to choose between competing or alternative deal terms in an M&A, especially if the deal terms don't have a clear dollar value attached to them, the founder does not know which one to choose or why. Essentially, without business objectives to guide them, the founders are unable to make a comprise they are satisfied with. When such a founder is then compelled to make the decision or they pass on it, they are never quite sure whether they got a good bargain or "won." The feeling of uncertainty doesn't always lose a founder the deal if they have the right team in place. The founder just doesn't enjoy, or learn from, the M&A experience. I don't want you to fall into such a trap, which is why I dedicated an entire chapter (Chapter 5) on how to seek business synergies through M&A like a buyer. Even if your goal is to get acquired for a glob of money, it will be an informed one and you will be able to make trade-offs more confidently.

Pace Yourself

If nothing else, I hope this book gave you an appreciation of how long and involved the M&A process can be for a company. By the time you get to a closing, you will have journeyed through a lot of milestones, hardships, and complexity. For a lot of founders who are used to pushing themselves to move fast and breaking things in order to build their start-up, they tend to apply the same strategy toward getting to a closing in an M&A. After all, founders are not strangers to long-term hardships and complexity.

However, that is not advisable for M&As. While an M&A is a move fast exercise, it is not tolerant of breaking things. Unlike a marriage where you can undo the marriage by divorce, you cannot untangle two companies who have already merged together. You will have to undertake one or more corporate transactions to mitigate the mistakes of a merger. In an M&A, the goal is to move fast but deliberately. Unlike the founder of an early-stage start-up where you are getting your hands dirty with the execution tasks, a lot of the leg work in an M&A is not done by you but by your hired advisors like the investment banker or M&A lawyer. Even with a full advisory team, there will be a lot of work on your plate to negotiate the high-value business deal terms, coordinate with the buyer, consult with your board of directors, shepherd your stockholders, and manage your employees (among many others). You will get the most out of an M&A if you are present in the moment to make the high-value and high-impact decisions that come at you. Taking care of your mental, physical, and emotional health, and that of your team, is key to successfully closing an M&A.

CONCLUSION

As you move forward from this book into undertaking M&A transactions in your business, my hope is that you do so with confidence. The M&A process is intricate and challenging, but with the knowledge and strategies you've gained, you are well-prepared to tackle it head-on. Whether you're planning to sell your company soon or simply want to be prepared for the future, the insights you've gained will serve you well.

Remember, the M&A journey is not just about the transaction itself – it's about achieving the best possible outcome for your future, whether that means financial security, personal fulfillment, or the continued success of your life's work. As you continue on your entrepreneurial journey, keep this book close as a resource and guide. And when the time comes, sell your company with confidence, knowing that you've done everything possible to achieve the best outcome.

Go forth fearlessly into the world of M&A, and let your vision guide you. Embrace the challenges, celebrate the successes, and always stay true to your goals. The journey ahead may be complex, but with the right mindset and preparation, you can achieve great things. I wish you the best of luck and look forward to hearing about your successes in the world of M&A.

Thank you, and good luck!

ABOUT THE AUTHOR

 Syeda Nazifa Nawroj, Esq., is an experienced corporate lawyer based in Silicon Valley. She specializes in advising founders, investors, and businesses on corporate governance and transactions, such as equity financings, loans, commercial deals and mergers and acquisitions (M&A). Over the better part of a decade, Syeda has represented small to midsize private companies at all stages of their formation, growth, and market exit. Syeda has a remarkable record of closing over thirty-five private M&A deals worth nearly $3 billion in total, and her expertise continues to grow.

Syeda is an immigrant to the United States, a mother, and a person of color. She was awarded a full scholarship at Mount Holyoke College and came to the United States for higher education. After college, Syeda self-funded her juris doctor degree from the prestigious New York University School of Law with private loans. At law school, Syeda served on the *NYU Law Review*. After law school, Syeda cut her teeth in corporate law at DLA Piper LLP (US), a global legal powerhouse, and later honed her expertise in M&A at Fenwick & West LLP, a prestigious, top-tier law firm. At Fenwick, Syeda focused on representing founders of technology and life-science companies in their strategic acquisitions during one of the high tides in private company M&A and grew to love it. Syeda's best-in-class legal training serves as a strong foundation and equips her to expertly support founders and businesses in her own law practice today.

Syeda represents clients across the United States and internationally in corporate transactions and other business matters. She aims to make high-value and high-impact corporate legal advice and services more accessible to small to midsize businesses through a unique combination of the smart use of technology, bespoke staffing, and flexible pricing. Her services are a particularly good offering for businesses that are looking to engage in small- and lower-middle-market M&A and strategic corporate transactions.

Over the years, Syeda has experienced and witnessed the challenges of completing a successful M&A transaction and how much more difficult it is for traditionally underserved founders (such as women, immigrants, BIPOC, and LGBTQ+ individuals). Syeda is driven by her passion to empower start-up founders, especially those from traditionally underrepresented and underserved backgrounds in corporate America, by making corporate law and M&A more accessible to them. This book is a part of her impassioned advocacy.

Syeda lives in Hollister, California, with her family. In her downtime, she enjoys hot yoga, vegetable gardening, and mentoring, constantly striving to give back to the many vibrant communities that support and shape her.

ABOUT DIFFERENCE PRESS

Difference Press is the publishing arm of The Author Incubator, an Inc. 500 award-winning company that helps business owners and executives grow their brand, establish thought leadership, and get customers, clients, and highly-paid speaking opportunities, through writing and publishing books.

While traditional publishers require that you already have a large following to guarantee they make money from sales to your existing list, our approach is focused on using a book to grow your following – even if you currently don't have a following. This is why we charge an up-front fee but never take a percentage of revenue you earn from your book.

☞ MORE THAN A COACH. MORE THAN A PUBLISHER. ✍

We work intimately and personally with each of our authors to develop a revenue-generating strategy for the book. By using a Lean Startup style methodology, we guarantee the book's success before we even start writing. We provide all the

technical support authors need with editing, design, marketing, and publishing, the emotional support you would get
from a book coach to help you manage anxiety and time
constraints, and we serve as a strategic thought partner engineering the book for success.

The Author Incubator has helped almost 2,000 entrepreneurs write, publish, and promote their non-fiction books. Our
authors have used their books to gain international media
exposure, build a brand and marketing following, get lucrative
speaking engagements, raise awareness of their product or
service, and attract clients and customers.

☞ ARE YOU READY TO WRITE A BOOK? ✍

As a client, we will work with you to make sure your book gets
done right and that it gets done quickly. The Author Incubator provides one-stop for strategic book consultation, author
coaching to manage writer's block and anxiety, full-service
professional editing, design, and self-publishing services, and
book marketing and launch campaigns. We sell this as one
package so our clients are not slowed down with contradictory
advice. We have a 99 percent success rate with nearly all of
our clients completing their books, publishing them, and
reaching bestseller status upon launch.

☞ APPLY NOW AND BE OUR NEXT SUCCESS STORY ✍

To find out if there is a significant ROI for you to write a book,
get on our calendar by completing an application at
www.TheAuthorIncubator.com/apply.

GIFTS FOR READER

I hope this guide has opened your eyes to the potential awaiting you with an M&A.

If you are looking for one-on-one help, please email me for a consultation at: contact@empowering.legal

Or, to gain access to the resources mentioned in this book, email book@empowering.legal.

If you scan the QR Code below, it will take you to the book's website at sellyourstartup.com, where you can also download the Gifts for Reader.

By doing so, you will receive the following:

- Sample standard initial due diligence request list
- Sample exclusivity agreement
- Sample confidentiality agreement

I look forward to hearing from you!

Made in the USA
Columbia, SC
27 November 2024

47258989R00163